At Issue

Self-Defense Laws

Other Books in the At Issue Series:

At Issue

I Self-Defense Laws

Tamara Thompson, Book Editor

GREENHAVEN PRESS
A part of Gale, Cengage Learning

GALE
CENGAGE Learning·

Farmington Hills, Mich • San Francisco • New York • Waterville, Maine
Meriden, Conn • Mason, Ohio • Chicago

Elizabeth Des Chenes, *Director, Content Strategy*
Cynthia Sanner, *Publisher*
Douglas Dentino, *Manager, New Product*

© 2014 Greenhaven Press, a part of Gale, Cengage Learning

WCN: 01-100-101

Gale and Greenhaven Press are registered trademarks used herein under license.

For more information, contact:
Greenhaven Press
27500 Drake Rd.
Farmington Hills, MI 48331-3535
Or you can visit our Internet site at gale.cengage.com

For product information and technology assistance, contact us at

Gale Customer Support, 1-800-877-4253
For permission to use material from this text or product, submit all requests online at
www.cengage.com/permissions

Further permissions questions can be emailed to permissionrequest@cengage.com

Articles in Greenhaven Press anthologies are often edited for length to meet page requirements. In addition, original titles of these works are changed to clearly present the main thesis and to explicitly indicate the author's opinion. Every effort is made to ensure that Greenhaven Press accurately reflects the original intent of the authors. Every effort has been made to trace the owners of copyrighted material.

Cover image copyright © Images.com/Corbis.

LIBRARY OF CONGRESS CATALOGING-IN-PUBLICATION DATA

Self-defense laws / Tamara Thompson, book editor.
    pages cm. -- (At issue)
    Summary: "At Issue: Self-Defense Laws: Books in this anthology series focus a wide range of viewpoints onto a single controversial issue, providing in-depth discussions by leading advocates, a quick grounding in the issues, and a challenge to critical thinking skills"-- Provided by publisher.
    Includes bibliographical references and index.
    ISBN 978-0-7377-6854-1 (hardback) -- ISBN 978-0-7377-6855-8 (paperback)
    1. Self-defense (Law)--United States. 2. Crime prevention--United States. I. Thompson, Tamara, editor of compilation.
    KF9246.S45 2013
    345.73'04--dc23
                                                          2013032062

Printed in the United States of America
1 2 3 4 5 6 7 18 17 16 15 14

Contents

Introduction

At its most fundamental level, self-defense is recognized as a natural right—a preexisting human right that everyone is inherently entitled to without it being specifically granted by law. That precept dates back to the ancient Roman Empire, which recognized an individual's right to defend himself and his property as morally proper and irrevocable by government.

An entry in the AD sixth-century Roman law code known as *Codex Justinianus* reads: "We grant to all persons the unrestricted power to defend themselves, so that it is proper to subject anyone . . . to immediate punishment in accordance with the authority granted to all. Let him suffer the death which he threatened and incur that which he intended."

That tenet helped shape seventeenth-century English Common Law, which framed the issue for the times and drafted laws based on the principle that "an Englishman's home is his castle." Modern American laws are direct descendants of these early justice systems, and the concepts of self-defense as a natural right and the inviolable sanctity of one's home endure in American legal statutes today.

But along with rights come responsibilities, and there are several important legal benchmarks that must be met in order to legitimize an action as self-defense—before physical force, up to and including deadly force, can be used against another person in a legally justified manner. The specifics of laws vary from state to state, but the long-held litmus test for an act to be deemed self-defense is that there must be a clear threat of imminent danger and no other option than to respond to it with force. The force used must not be excessive, and the actions must be what a "reasonable person" would do under similar circumstances. A person may not use force to avoid future harm, however; the peril must be truly immediate. Historically, American self-defense laws have also included a "duty to retreat," that is, a requirement that one must retreat from a conflict rather than respond with violence if it is possible and safe to do so. In recent years, however, those requirements have changed significantly, and the right to self-defense has been expanded in several important ways.

Two relatively new types of laws are the driving force behind this expansion of self-defense rights in states nationwide. One is known as Castle Doctrine laws and the other, Stand Your Ground (SYG) laws. Based on the old concepts from English Common Law, Castle Doctrine laws strengthen the right to self-defense by eliminating the duty to retreat from a threat in one's own home or on one's own property. Building on that idea, so-called SYG laws extend the Castle Doctrine concept to any place where a person has a right to be, such as one's car, workplace, or a public sidewalk. Often called "Shoot First" or "Make My Day" laws, these controversial self-defense statutes essentially allow someone who feels threatened to stand their ground and respond with force rather than retreat, even if they are safely able to do so. The first explicit Castle Doctrine law was adopted in Florida in 2005, and twenty-four states now have Castle laws or even stronger SYG variations of them, thanks largely to the efforts of the National Rifle Association (NRA).

A 2012 statement available on the NRA website maintains:

The vast majority of states do not impose a "duty to retreat" and most Americans support laws that clarify that Common Law, common-sense right. It empowers lawful people to defend themselves, and deters would-be murderers, rapists and robbers. It's a natural right. No law "gives" it or can take it away. It's yours. It works. And its only alternative—the idea that distant, disinterested third parties can dictate after the fact that "you must retreat"—will never be accepted by the American people. For these reasons, the National Rifle Association will work to protect self-defense laws on the books and advocate for their passage in those states that do not fully respect this fundamental right.

Critics, however, say that although such laws indeed protect good citizens when confronted by individuals with malevolent intent, they are also vaguely written and poorly enforced, so they are frequently exploited by people who wrongly claim self-defense to excuse their violent actions. An additional hurdle in such cases is that the burden is on the court to disprove claims of self-defense rather than on defendants to prove that they acted legitimately.

Those are the key issues surrounding the controversial 2012 Florida case in which neighborhood watch volunteer George Zimmerman shot seventeen-year-old Trayvon Martin to death after following and confronting him because he thought he looked suspicious. Prosecutors say Zimmerman deliberately pursued and murdered the teen; Zimmerman claims he shot Martin in self-defense during a physical struggle in which he feared for his life. Zimmerman was armed with a handgun; Martin was unarmed, carrying only a can of iced tea and a bag of candy. The case garnered national headlines and generated intense public outcry because Zimmerman was not immediately arrested and charged in the killing; the state's SYG law did not permit his arrest during the investigation. Zimmerman was, however, eventually jailed and charged with second-degree murder. His trial began in June 2013, and relying on Florida's statute of self-defense as the basis of his case, he was eventually acquitted of both second-degree murder and the lesser charge of manslaughter.

Another high-profile self-defense case that played out in the courts in 2013 was that of Jodi Arias, who faced first-degree murder charges in Arizona for stabbing her ex-boyfriend Travis Alexander twenty-seven times, slitting his throat from ear to ear, and shooting him in the forehead. At first, Arias denied any knowledge of the killing, then blamed it on "masked intruders." Finally, she claimed that she acted in self-defense, saying Alexander had been physically abusing her.

"By alleging domestic abuse, Arias can portray herself as the 'real' victim," writes Colette McIntyre, associate editor for TheJaneDough.com, a popular website for professional women. "Under the guise of self-defense, her attack may be interpreted as justifiable. If Arias is in fact lying about the abuse, she is making a mockery of real domestic abuse victims."

Indeed, women who defend themselves against their abusers find themselves in a unique position in the criminal justice system. Building on increased awareness about violence against women in the 1970s, researchers identified what is now commonly known as Battered Woman Syndrome (BWS), a term that describes the difficult-to-escape cycle of violence particular to abusive relationships. "Thanks to the growing research on BWS and the tireless work of domestic abuse organizations," writes McIntyre, "courts are now more likely to recognize evidence of domestic violence in support of self-defense claims." However, she continues, "using a self-defense claim as a courtroom gambit completely undermines public confidence in true allegations of domestic abuse. Every defense that falsely invokes justifiable homicide worsens the plight of women who are charged with killing their abusers."

And there are many. According to the National Clearinghouse for the Defense of Battered Women (NCDBW), 90 percent of the women currently imprisoned for killing men were battered by those same men; a shocking 42 percent of those women claimed their actions were in self-defense, but they were convicted anyway. The NCDBW also cites FBI figures that show women convicted of such killings are typically sentenced to significantly longer prison terms than men who kill their mates, a statistic many say raises serious questions about the fairness of the criminal justice system.

Like Castle Doctrine and SYG laws, Battered Woman Syndrome can be an authentic justification for the use of deadly force in self-defense, or it can be exploited as a shady excuse for unwarranted acts of violence. Jodi Arias was convicted of first-degree murder on May 8, 2013, and may face the death penalty.

The authors in *At Issue: Self-Defense Laws* present a wide range of viewpoints about the various legal issues related to self-defense and whether modern self-defense statutes are ultimately in the best interest of justice in a democratic society.

1

Overview: The Legal Principles of Self-Defense

Richard Klein

Richard Klein is the Bruce Gould Distinguished Professor of Law at Touro Law School in New York City.

There are several important legal principles involved in a legitimate act of self-defense. Most importantly, there must be a clear threat of imminent danger with no option available other than to respond to it with force. Some states require a threatened person to retreat if possible, while others allow individuals to stand their ground. The force used for self-defense must not be excessive, and the actions must be what a "reasonable person" would do under similar circumstances. A person may not use force to avoid future harm; the danger must be immediate or else there is no valid claim of self-defense. If a person uses force because he incorrectly believes that such a response is necessary for self-defense, the doctrine of imperfect self-defense can reduce but not eliminate any resulting criminal charges. In self-defense cases, the burden is on the state to disprove claims of self-defense rather than on defendants to prove that they acted legitimately.

A valid and appropriate use of self-defense justifies the use of force against another, even when such force results in death. But the force used must have been absolutely necessary in order to protect oneself, it cannot have been used as form

Richard Klein, "Race and the Doctrine of Self Defense: The Role of Race in Determining the Proper Use of Force to Protect Oneself," *Journal of Race, Gender and Ethnicity*, vol. 4, no. 3, November 2009. Copyright © 2009 by Richard Klein. All rights reserved. Reproduced by permission.

of self-help or as a display of vindictiveness to retaliate against an individual or a group which has treated the accused in negative, hostile ways in the past. When Bernhard Goetz shot at 4 black youths in a subway car [in New York in 1984], was it because he truly believed such an action was necessary in order to protect himself from the infliction of serious harm? And if indeed such *was* his personal belief, is that sufficient to justify his shootings or does the law require that the belief be a reasonable one supported by an objective standard? When John White shot and killed Daniel Cicciaro [in New York in 2006] did he have a valid self-defense based, in part, on his knowledge of the lynchings and attacks on blacks in the southern parts of the U.S. in prior decades?

A Defense of Necessity

Self-defense is classified as a necessity defense, the individual claiming the defense must have had no available option but to attack the person who created the threat. And, as the Model Penal Code [a document designed as a model for standardizing criminal law across the United States] makes clear, the force that was used must have been "*immediately* necessary for the purpose of protecting himself." It is generally required that there must have been an overt act by the threatening individual that presented an imminent danger to the person who is claiming self-defense. Any desire by an individual to use force to punish someone else for conduct others of his race may have previously engaged in, voids the claim of self-defense. A vigilante who feels the need to take the law into his own hands is a criminal. The desire to retaliate to make amends for past wrongs may be understandable, but our criminal justice system speaks clearly and in one voice: No citizen is to act as judge and jury and inflict punishment. Enforcement of the law and dealing with those who are violating the laws are for the police and the police alone.

Self-defense has been recognized as a valid defense throughout the history of our laws. Blackstone's *Commentaries* [an eighteenth-century text on the Common Law of England written by Sir William Blackstone] reports that "for the one uniform principle that runs through our own, and all other laws, seems to be this: that where a crime, in itself capital, is endeavored to be committed by force, it is lawful to repel that force by the death of the party attempting." The defense applied to a threat of assault, not just a potential killing: "The defense . . . is that whereby a man may protect himself from an assault, or the like, in the course of a sudden brawl or quarrel, by killing him who assaults him." And in New York, the penal statutes have, since 1829, codified the common law right to use physical force in self-defense.

Deadly physical force can be used only to defend oneself against the use of deadly physical force of another.

Defenses vs. Excuses

Self-defense is generally considered to be, as it is in New York State, a Justification defense. Whereas defenses, which are labeled as Justifications, absolve the individual actor from any criminal liability for his conduct, the defenses considered to be Excuses have traditionally not led to the defendant's release from liability. But the use of the phrase "justification" ought not to be interpreted as the criminal justice system's approval of what had been done, but only that the conduct engaged in was understandable and will be tolerated without sanction. The presence of justification does not in any way negate an element of the crime with which the defendant has been charged.

The New York State Justification statute provides that an individual may use "physical force upon another person when and to the extent he or she reasonably believes such to be necessary to defend himself, herself or a third person from what he or she reasonably believes to be the use or imminent use of unlawful physical force by such other person[.]" Deadly physical force can be used only to defend oneself against the use of deadly physical force of another. It may at times become an issue for the jury to determine whether the actor was truly confronted with the use of physical force that would be considered to be "deadly." The New York State Penal Law defines such force as constituting "physical force which, under the circumstances in which it is used, as readily capable of causing death or other serious physical injury." As we shall see, the distinction between the accused use of deadly versus non-deadly force is crucial as to the obligation by the defendant to have retreated prior to the use of force.

The Model Penal Code emphasizes the import of the defendant's intentions when assessing whether or not he was using deadly force: "A threat to cause death or serious bodily harm, by the production of a weapon or otherwise, as long as the actor's purpose is limited to creating an apprehension that he will use deadly physical force if necessary, does not constitute deadly force." The New York Penal Laws, however, do not provide for such an interpretation based upon an evaluation of the motives of the individual who threatens another with the use of deadly physical force.

For self-defense, the prosecutor has the burden of disproving the claim of self-defense beyond a reasonable doubt.

The Problem of Imminent Threat

The most problematic requirement for one who is claiming self-defense is the need to show that the threat that was being responded to was an "imminent" one. Imminent is generally thought of as immediate; if the threat confronting the accused had been the use of future force, there was no immediate threat and self-defense does not apply. If one acts in a preemptive manner to avoid even certain harm that will occur at a later date, self-defense is inapplicable. In this respect, the law of self-defense is analogous to the requirements for the use of any other necessity defense. . . .

An additional requirement for a valid self-defense is that the force used by the actor not have been excessive. Whereas it may have been appropriate and justified for an individual to have used deadly force to protect himself, was the force used in a manner that was disproportionate to the threat? Would a use of lesser force have accomplished the goal of protecting oneself? . . .

An All-or-Nothing Defense

If any one of the elements for the justification of self-defense fails, the defense is not valid. The threat against the individual must have been one with the potential of causing serious physical injury, the threat must have been an immediate one and the force used in defense must not have been excessive. Once the threat no longer exists, the necessity to use force has ended. In *People v. Kruger*, the court held that the right to use self-defense had terminated once the attacker had been shot and incapacitated because there was no longer any threat. The second shot, which was fired, therefore, was not done in self-defense.

In New York State, self-defense is deemed to be an ordinary defense. Defenses, on the other hand, that are considered to be Excuses and not Justification defenses are labeled affirmative defenses. The distinction is one of great import. For self-defense, the prosecutor has the burden of disproving the claim of self-defense beyond a reasonable doubt. Whenever the defendant has submitted evidence of self-defense, the court must then rule whether, as a matter of law, the defendant's claimed facts if established would constitute self-defense. The Court is required to view the evidence in the light which is most favorable to the accused. There is no common law approach in New York to the defense, the requirements of Penal Law § 35.15 control. If the defendant has raised a colorable claim of self-defense, the judge has the obligation to instruct the jury as to the requirements needed to establish the defense. The justification charge that is required is to include an explanation of the burden of the prosecution to disprove the validity of the defense. The failure of the trial judge in New York to give the jury a justification charge is not to be deemed as mere harmless error.

Some states hold it is not reversible error for the trial judge to fail to give the charge for self-defense if the defendant has not made a request for the jury instruction or has not presented evidence indicating self-defense. In California, it is considered to be reversible error to fail to give the charge for imperfect self-defense when evidence has been introduced to support the defense. Where self-defense is deemed to be an affirmative defense, the defendant may raise the defense only if he or the State presents evidence in support of the necessary elements of the defense.

The imperfect self-defense applies when the defendant did have an honest belief that he was being threatened, but such belief was not considered ... to have been a reasonable one.

The Burden of Proof

The burden for proving self-defense also varies according to jurisdiction. In some states, self-defense is designated as an affirmative defense that places the burden on the defendant to prove he or she acted in self-defense by a preponderance of the evidence. The United States Supreme Court, in *Martin v. Ohio*, upheld the constitutionality of requiring the defendant to prove self-defense by preponderance for the evidence; such a requirement was found not to violate Due Process. Most jurisdictions follow the New York approach: self-defense must be disproved by the State beyond a reasonable doubt once evidence is introduced relating to self-defense. The New Jersey Supreme Court in *State v. Gardner*, however, has ruled that it is erroneous to place the burden on the defendant: "Once [the] proof appears either in the State's case or defendant's case in support of an allegation of self-defense, the State has the burden of proving that the defense is untrue. And that the State must do so beyond a reasonable doubt." Similarly, a California jury instruction in *People v. Cornett* regarding self-defense was determined to be erroneous when the burden was placed on the defendant. The jury should have been instructed that the homicide is to be found to have been justified if the evidence as self-defense raises a reasonable doubt of guilt. South Carolina, however, departs from the majority and requires the defendant to prove by the greater weight of the evidence that he acted in self-defense.

Courts Wrestle with How to Set Standards

Courts and legislatures throughout the country have wrestled with the standard to be used in assessing whether or not the accused acted reasonably when he concluded that he was being threatened with the imminent use of deadly physical force. Should there be a subjective standard, wherein self-defense would be warranted as long as that particular individual believed he was threatened? Or, should the standard be an objective one, and only if a reasonable person would have felt threatened would the defense be appropriate?. . .

Imperfect Self-Defense

Some states have attempted to deal with the objective/subjective dilemma by creating what is referred to as an imperfect self-defense. The perfect self-defense applies if a reasonable person in the defendant's position would have believed he was in imminent danger. Such a defense justifies the response of the defendant to the threat and an acquittal of the charges is to result. The imperfect self-defense applies when the defendant did have an honest belief that he was being threatened, but such belief was not considered by the trier of fact to have been a reasonable one. The impact of such an imperfect self-defense is not to acquit the defendant, but rather serves to act in mitigation. A murder charge will typically be reduced to manslaughter if an imperfect self-defense is found.

The most common instance that leads to the imperfect self-defense charge is when the defendant's perception of the threat meets the test under the subjective prong and not the objective prong. If there is no such a charge informing jurors of the existence of an imperfect self-defense, the defendant will be guilty of murder because the "perfect" self-defense will fail. For example, in *State v. Shaw*, the defendant wanted a jury instruction for imperfect self-defense, however the state of Vermont does not allow for this charge and a murder conviction resulted. California, however, recognizes imperfect self-defense to be a mitigating factor if it is found that the defendant had a sincere belief that he or she was in imminent danger of death or serious physical injury but this belief was determined to have been unreasonable. In *Christian S.*, alleged members of a California gang harassed the defendant for over a year, and in response, the fearful defendant started carrying a pistol. On one occasion, there was a dispute concerning damage to a truck, and the defendant drew his weapon as the victim continued to approach him; the victim taunted the defendant and dared him to shoot. The defendant shot and killed the victim from twenty feet away. The defense claimed that however unreasonable the killing might appear to be, the defendant did have an honest fear of imminent death or serious physical injury which therefore served to negate the element of malice required for murder. The defense contended that at most a conviction of voluntary manslaughter would be warranted. The California Supreme Court held that a charge of imperfect self-defense should be permitted. The Court held that if the defendant honestly believed that he was shooting because of an imminent fear of death or serious physical injury, the murder charge should be reduced to manslaughter because even though the shooting was intentional, the imperfect self-defense negated the element of malice required for a conviction of murder.

Mitigation vs. Justification

In Pennsylvania, the statute is clear: "[A] person who intentionally or knowingly kills an individual commits voluntary manslaughter if at the time of the killing he believes the circumstances to be such that, if they existed, would justify the killing . . . but his belief is unreasonable." The Model Penal Code allows for mitigation but not justification of a murder charge if the defendant had a subjective but mistaken belief regarding a threat and was "reckless or negligent in having such belief or acquiring or failing to acquire any knowledge or belief which is material to the justifiability of his use of force. . . ."

Some states permit an imperfect self-defense jury instruction to be given to the jury when the defendant fails to meet one element required for a "perfect" self-defense. In *Swann v. U.S.*, the D.C. Court of Appeals allowed the charge when the defendant was the initial aggressor (which negates the applicability of self-defense) but acted due to a subjective fear of imminent death or serious physical injury. The Court determined that "a defendant's actual belief both in the presence of danger and in the need to resort to force, even if one or both beliefs be objectively unreasonable, constitutes a legally sufficient mitigating factor to warrant a finding of voluntary manslaughter rather than second degree murder."

The Duty to Retreat

New York State law imposes a major restriction on the use of self-defense. An individual cannot use deadly force to defend oneself if [he or she] "knows that with complete safety to oneself and others he or she may avoid the necessity of so doing by retreating." . . .

The doctrine of retreat can be traced back to English common law. Deadly force was permitted to be used only when an individual had his "back to the wall." It was initially required that one had to have attempted to flee the scene altogether; if that proved impossible, one must attempt to get as far away as possible from the enemy—until one's back was up against the wall. It was only at that time, were the threat to still be continuing, that one may use force in self-defense. The long-standing common law exception to the obligation to retreat if assault—and not murder—was the charge against the defendant, was changed in New York by statute requiring retreat before self-defense in any instance could be claimed.

The National Rifle Association has aggressively lobbied for abolition of the retreat requirement.

The provisions of the Model Penal Code, which relate to retreat, are virtually identical to those in New York. There are, however, great difficulties in the application of the retreat doctrine. First, the test is a subjective one. An actor is required to have *known* that he had the option of a completely safe retreat. But how can the prosecutor be expected to show that the defendant actually had such knowledge and that, therefore, the use of deadly force was not necessary? The fact-finders are not to apply a reasonable person standard and assume, therefore, that this defendant knew of the retreat option. Any charge to the jury that indicates that an objective standard is to be used is improper and if a conviction results subsequent to such an instruction by the court, it will be overturned. Certainly, if the defendant were to testify at trial, he will claim that he never believed that he could just leave the scene with complete safety.

The Standard of Complete Safety

And, indeed it is "complete" safety that is required. In *State v. Anderson*, the Supreme Court of Connecticut overturned the defendant's conviction because the judge's instructions to the jury had failed to use the words "complete safety." In the common situation where the aggressor possesses a gun and is threatening its use, how can a jury determine that the defendant knew he could retreat from the threat in complete safety? Because, in part, of these practical concerns, there has recently been a steady trend in the number of states which are abolishing the retreat requirement.

It was in Ohio, in 1876, where the "true man" concept originated. A "true man" is not a coward who retreats from a confrontation; a "true man" stands his ground and uses the force required to meet the threat. It has not been the courts that have led the way to the departures from the requirement of retreat. In a two-year period, the legislatures of fifteen states have enacted what are commonly referred to as "stand your ground laws." The National Rifle Association has aggressively lobbied for abolition of the retreat requirement and these efforts have led a total of 30 states in the years 2005–2007 to consider changing their laws on self-defense. A spokesperson for the National Rifle Association justified its support for the anti-retreat legislation in that law-abiding citizens should know that "if they make a decision to save their lives in the split second they are being attacked, the law is on their side."

Stand Your Ground Laws

The new statutes are often shaped by the "Stand Your Ground" laws enacted in Florida in 2005. The new legislation is clear. If an individual is attacked in a place where he has a right to be, then he has "no duty to retreat and has the right to stand his or her ground and meet force with force, including deadly force if he or she reasonably believes it is necessary to prevent death or great bodily harm to himself or herself or another."

Even in those states such as New York that still adhere to the retreat doctrine, there is an exception provided for one who is in his own home at the time of the threat. Justice [Benjamin N.] Cardozo, in the 1914 case of *People v. Tomlins*, explained the rationale: "It is not now and never has been the law that a man assailed in his own dwelling is bound to retreat. If assailed there, he may stand his ground, and resist the attack. He is under no duty to take to the fields and the highways, a fugitive from his own home."

In New York State, as is true in virtually every state as well as the Model Penal Code, the initial aggressor in the conflict cannot claim a justified use of self-defense. Whereas there often is not a clarification within the penal codes as to what exactly designates one the initial aggressor, it is generally accepted that the person who is at fault for provoking the confrontation is considered to be the initial aggressor. Another common formulation of this restriction on the use of self-defense was stated by the court in *Nowlin v. United States*: "Appellant had no legitimate claim to the defense of self-defense since he had voluntarily placed himself in a position which he could reasonably expect would result in violence."

Every state in the country allows for an accused to claim that he was justified when using force, including the use of deadly force, in order to protect himself from danger. The Supreme Court has, in the controversial case of *District of Columbia v. Heller*, reinforced the availability the right to act in self-defense when it ruled that the Second Amendment of the Constitution affords the individual the right to use and possess a firearm for self-defense. Whereas states may and do vary considerably in their requirements for an individual to fully and properly exercise such a claim, there is some degree of uniformity regarding the primary basis for self-defense.

It is almost always the case that in order to show that the use of deadly force was warranted, an individual must show that he acted under a reasonable belief that such force was required and necessary in order to protect himself from the unlawful use of force by another. The threat itself must have been one involving the *imminent* use of deadly force; if not, then the accused should have pursued options other than the use of force. Furthermore, the amount of force utilized must have been proportionate to the threat; once an amount of force is used that was more than was needed to repel the threat, the individual is no longer acting out of self-defense. It is all too common that someone who *initially* is acting strictly to protect himself, may then continue to use force that is excessive and unjustifiable. Such concerns arise with some frequency when women who claim to have been battered utilize the battered woman syndrome form of self-defense.

Perhaps the aspect of the law of self-defense that most varies from state to state is presented by a fact pattern where, although a particular defendant *did* perceive there to be a legitimate threat, a reasonable person would not have felt threatened. In some states, such defendant would not be able to claim self-defense, whereas in other jurisdictions such a claim would be warranted. Additionally, some states have dealt with this difficult area by the creation of the *imperfect* self-defense.

Self-defense laws are surely one of the most controversial aspects of our criminal justice system, as the debate regarding George Zimmerman/Trayvon Martin and the Stand-Your-Ground law in Florida exemplifies. Important policy concerns remain, and in our efforts to diminish crime in a society where gun possession and horrific shootings seem to be occurring with ever-increasing frequency, the proper role of our laws of self-defense will remain under well-needed scrutiny.

2

Self-Defense Is a Natural Right

David B. Kopel

David B. Kopel is an associate policy analyst at the Cato Institute, a libertarian think tank. He is also research director at the Independence Institute and adjunct professor of advanced constitutional law at Denver University's Sturm College of Law. He has written twelve books, including The Samurai, the Mountie, and the Cowboy: Should America Adopt the Gun Controls of Other Democracies?

The District of Columbia v. Heller *case was a landmark legal decision in which the US Supreme Court ruled for the first time that the Second Amendment of the Constitution protects an individual's right to possess a firearm for a traditionally lawful purpose, such as self-defense. The 2008 decision upheld that right in an individual's home and within "federal enclaves" such as the District of Columbia, which the court found had unconstitutionally restricted gun possession within its boundaries. Part of the basis for the court's decision in the* Heller *case was the concept of natural law—a preexisting natural right that everyone is inherently entitled to without it being specifically granted by legal statute. The right of self-defense is a natural law that is guaranteed by the Second Amendment, not granted by it.*

One of the most important elements of the *District of Columbia v. Heller* decision is the natural law. Analysis of natural law in *Heller* shows why Justice [John P.] Stevens' dissent is clearly incorrect, and illuminates a crucial weakness in Justice [Stephen] Breyer's dissent. The constitutional recognition of the natural law right of self-defense has important implications for American law, and for foreign and international law.

Heller reaffirms a point made in the 1876 *Cruikshank* case [which dealt with how the Bill of Rights applies to state governments]. The right to arms (unlike, say, the right to grand jury indictment) is *not* a right which is granted by the Constitution. It is a pre-existing natural right which is recognized and protected by the Constitution:

> [I]t has always been widely understood that the Second Amendment, like the First and Fourth Amendments, codified a *pre-existing* right. The very text of the Second Amendment implicitly recognizes the pre-existence of the right and declares only that it "shall not be infringed." As we said in *United States v. Cruikshank*, "[t]his is not a right granted by the Constitution. Neither is it in any manner dependent upon that instrument for its existence. The Second [A]mendment declares that it shall not be infringed...."

The Predecessor to the Second Amendment

As *Heller* pointed out, the 1689 English Declaration of Right (informally known as the English Bill of Rights) was a "predecessor to our Second Amendment." According to the Declaration: "the [s]ubjects which are Protestants may have [a]rms for their [d]efence suitable to their [c]onditions and as allowed by [l]aw." The Convention Parliament which wrote the Declaration of Right stated that the right to arms for defense was a "true[, ancient,] and indubitable Right[]." Yet, as [constitutional scholar] Joyce Malcolm has detailed, 1689 was the first time that the right to arms had been formally protected by a positive enactment of English law.

The explanation is simple. The Convention Parliament did not believe that it was creating new rights, but simply recognizing established ones. Although previous Parliaments had not enacted a statute specifically to protect the right of armed self-defense, British case law since 1330 had long recognized an absolute right to use deadly force against home invaders. The right to self-defense itself, along with its necessary implication of the right to use appropriate arms for self-defense, was considered to be firmly established by natural law.

Thus, *Heller* quoted Blackstone's treatise [*Commentaries on the Laws of England*, an eighteenth-century text written by Sir William Blackstone] (which was by far the most influential legal treatise in the early American republic) explaining that the Declaration of Right protected "'the natural right of resistance and self-preservation,'" which was effectuated by "'the right of having and using arms for self-preservation and defence.'"

The natural law basis of the right to armed self-defense is part of the original public meaning of the Second Amendment.

Citations from Other Cases

Some other parts of the *Heller* opinion include citations to sources describing the right of armed self-defense as a "natural" or "inherent" right. The majority writes that "Justice James Wilson interpreted the Pennsylvania Constitution's arms-bearing right, for example, as a recognition of the natural right of defense 'of one's person or house'—what he called the law of 'self preservation.'"

Likewise quoted with approval is the 1846 Georgia Supreme Court decision *Nunn v. State*, which "construed the Second Amendment as protecting the '*natural* right of self-defence.'" Similarly, "A New York article of April 1769 said that '[i]t is a natural right which the people have reserved to themselves, confirmed by the Bill of Rights, to keep arms for their own defence.'"

Thus, the *Heller* opinion concludes: "[a]s the quotations earlier in this opinion demonstrate, the inherent right of self-defense has been central to the Second Amendment right." *Heller's* recognition of self-defense as a natural right was consistent with the same view in *The Federalist*, in most state constitutions, and in case law from before the Civil War to modern times.

The Roots of Natural Law

Although some modern scholars deny that natural law exists, there is no dispute that the Founders strongly believed in it. In a constitutional sense, the natural law basis of the right to armed self-defense is part of the original public meaning of the Second Amendment. That human rights were inherent, and not granted by government, was, after all, the basis on which the nation was created: "We hold these truths to be self-evident . . . that [all men] are endowed by their Creator with certain unalienable Rights. . . ."

"Natural law" as a term of legal art was originally based on Catholic legal thought. In the twelfth century, [jurist Johannes] Gratian's "Treatise of the Discordant Canons" consolidated and synthesized disparate sources in various canon laws (church laws). He began with an explanation of natural law:

> Natural law is common to all nations because it exists everywhere through natural instinct, not because of any enactment. For example: the union of men and women, the succession and rearing of children, the common possession of all things, the identical liberty of all, or the acquisition of things that are taken from the heavens, earth, or sea, as well as the return of a thing deposited or of money entrusted to one, and the repelling of violence by force. This, and anything similar, is never regarded as unjust but is held to be natural and equitable.

Gratian's formulation of the natural right of "repelling violence by force" was similar to an expression of the same principle in Roman law.

In the five centuries from Gratian to the American Constitution, the concept of natural law, including natural rights, was developed by Catholic scholars such as Thomas Aquinas, Francisco de Vitoria, Juan de Mariana, and Francisco Suárez (who called self-defense "the greatest of all rights"). From the personal right of self-defense against lone criminals, they derived the people's right of self-defense against criminal, tyrannical governments.

The Declaration of Independence affirms that governments are created for the purpose of protecting natural rights.

Important Writers

Few Americans were familiar with these Catholic scholars, except for Aquinas. The Anglo-Americans learned the language of natural rights, including the natural right of self-defense, from Protestant thinkers who had adopted the Catholic self-defense theories. The first of these writers were the persecuted Protestants of sixteenth-century France and England, including Theodore Beza, Peter Martyr Vermigli, and Christopher Goodman. For the Americans, the most influential were John Ponet, author of *A Shorte Treatise of Politike Power* (1556), and the pseudonymous Stephanus Junius Brutus, who wrote *Vindiciae Contra Tyrannos* (Vindication Against Tyrants) in 1579. According to [founding father] John Adams, *Vindiciae* was one of the leading books by which England's and America's "present liberties have been established." Adams wrote that there were three key periods in English history where scholars addressed the problems of tyranny and the proper structure of governments. The first of these, according to Adams, was the English reformation; next, when John Ponet put forth "all the essential principles of liberty, which were afterward dilated on by Sidney and Locke."

The Founders were also familiar with the great writers of international law, who based their entire system on the foundation of the natural right of self-defense. Hugo Grotius, the most important writer of all time in international law, built the laws of international warfare by extrapolation from the natural right of personal defense. Samuel von Pufendorf, who extended and elaborated Grotius's work on international law and political philosophy, called self-defense the foundation of civilized society.

The Declaration of Independence affirms that governments are created for the purpose of protecting natural rights. Accordingly, a necessary feature of a legitimate government will be the protection of natural rights. As the Supreme Court explained in *Cruikshank*, the right to assemble and the right to keep and bear arms are, each, "found wherever civilization exists." Although personal self-defense is not specifically mentioned in the Declaration of Independence, that natural right is the intellectual foundation, in Western philosophy, of the right of the people to defend all their natural rights by using force to overthrow a tyrant.

Natural Right and the Stevens' Dissent

Justice Stevens' dissent does about as well as possible, given the facts available, on issues such as how much weight to give to the Second Amendment's preamble, and whether "bear arms" must necessarily mean the carrying of guns *only* while in military service. Throughout the opinion, he argues passionately for his interpretation, although that interpretation requires a very selective view of the evidence; the dissent is like the argument that a sheet of paper has only one dimension, because if you look at it from just the right angle, it appears to be a straight line. Vast amounts of evidence have to be willfully ignored. For example, one treatise by Justice [Joseph] Story describes the Second Amendment in terms which are, at least arguably, not necessarily incompatible with

Stevens' militia-only view. But another treatise by Story, which was quoted by the majority, describes the Second Amendment in terms which fit the *Heller* majority's view, and which are plainly contrary to the Stevens militia-only theory. The majority opinion discusses both treatises, but Stevens writes at length about the first treatise, ignores the existence of the second treatise, and provides no explanation for having done so.

The Second Amendment does not purport to grant a right, but instead declares that "the right . . . shall not be infringed." Thus, the Second Amendment guarantees a pre-existing right.

Justice Stevens dismisses the English Declaration of Right, and Blackstone's description thereof, by contending that they addressed issues which were not of concern to the Founders, who according to Stevens were only thinking about the state ratification debates involving state vs. federal powers over the militia. Stevens' view is contrary to that of [founding father] James Madison, the author of the Second Amendment. In Madison's notes for his speech introducing the Bill of Rights into the House of Representatives, he described the arms rights amendment as remedying two crucial defects in the English Declaration of Right: that the right included only the Protestant population, and that the right was, as a statutory enactment, efficacious against the King, but not against the actions of later Parliaments.

Justice Stevens Misses the Mark

But even without reference to Madison's notes, the Stevens theory that the Second Amendment does not include the right of self-defense simply collapses when one gets to the word "the."

The Second Amendment does not purport to grant a right, but instead declares that "the right . . . shall not be infringed."

Thus, the Second Amendment guarantees a pre-existing right. The *Heller* majority says so, and Stevens concedes the point. What was that pre-existing right? There are only two possibilities. One, as explicated by [Justice Antonin] Scalia (consistent with Madison), is that the right is the English/Blackstone/ natural right of arms for self-defense. Stevens, however, contends that "the" right is the right to serve in an armed militia. Only if he is correct about this point can his dissent as a whole be correct that the Second Amendment is purely about a right to have arms while in militia service.

There is not a shred of evidence from 1789, or from anytime before 1789, that militia service was a "right." As Justice Scalia pointed out, the Stevens claim that "the" pre-existing right in the Second Amendment was a pre-existing right to service in the militia is unsupported by any evidence. There is simply no document or other source, from the eighteenth, seventeenth, or sixteenth centuries (or indeed from any century until the twenty-first, when the claim was invented as part of the *Heller* litigation) that the Second Amendment was preceded somewhere in Anglo-American law by a right to serve in the militia, or to have arms solely while in the militia. Rather, this novel theory appears in the *Heller* amicus brief filed by the Brady Center. The brief, too, is unadorned by any citation for its claim.

Natural Right and the Breyer Dissent

Most of the Breyer dissent lays out an interest-balancing test, in which Justice Breyer argues that there is *some* social science evidence in favor of the D.C. handgun ban, and therefore a judge cannot say as a matter of law that the ban is unconstitutional. A crucial step in that interest-balancing test is the weight of the interest on each side. Justice Breyer points out that preservation of arms ownership for use in a citizen militia was a major concern of the Second Amendment. Accordingly, he disputes the majority's statement that the right of self-defense is "central" to the Second Amendment, and that the "core" of the Second Amendment is armed self-defense of the home.

> The Founders could see that self-defense had been protected under the laws of Ancient Rome and Ancient Greece, and from the very inception of the Hebrew nation.

Justice Scalia responded by explaining why interest-balancing was inappropriate for a core constitutional right, but he did not directly address Breyer's question about why self-defense should be considered part of the core in the first place. However, the answer is fairly clear from the natural law perspective which is incorporated in the majority opinion. Blackstone describes the right to personal defensive arms (protected, but not created by the 1689 English Declaration of Right) as a "natural" right. Other sources in the majority opinion make the same point that the Second Amendment protects a "natural" right.

Laws Protect Existing Rights

Even if balancing were appropriate, Justice Breyer's scales are inaccurate, because they underweigh the importance of self-defense. Surely nothing could be more fundamental than a natural right. The Declaration of Independence, after all, did not begin with a statement of the importance of rights which were created by government (e.g., the right of a citizen to be assisted by his nation's consular offices when he is traveling in a foreign country). Rather, the Declaration starts with natural, inherent rights, and states that the very purpose of government is to protect these rights. By the Declaration's principles, the time that is most appropriate for rigorous judicial review is when a government infringes on one of the natural rights which the very government was established to protect.

From Grotius, Pufendorf, and many other sources, the Founders could see that self-defense had been protected under the laws of Ancient Rome and Ancient Greece, and from the very inception of the Hebrew nation. The historical episodes when the right of armed self-defense was endangered—the persecution of the disarmed Huguenots in France, the gun bans of the power-mad Stuart monarchs in England, the 1775 confiscation of privately-owned firearms from the people of Boston by General Gage's army—were precisely the episodes of tyranny which the Founders aimed to ensure would never again take place in the United States of America. From the Founders' perspective, the right to arms truly was found "wherever civilization exists."

Implications for American Law

Self-defense has generally been highly regarded by the American public, and [Fordham University law professor] Nicholas Johnson has persuasively argued that self-defense is the epitome of an unenumerated Ninth Amendment right. In contrast, some commentary has denigrated self-defense as a privilege, not a right.

Heller moves self-defense from the shadowy limbo of the Ninth Amendment into the bright uplands of the Second Amendment. It is now beyond dispute in an American court that self-defense is an inherent right, and that it is protected by the United States Constitution.

The constitutional history of the right of self-defense is similar to that of the right of association. The right of association is not formally stated in the Constitution. But it is easy to see how if the right did not exist, many of the core purposes of the First Amendment might be defeated. For example, if people could not voluntarily associate in groups such as the NAACP, then their practical ability to petition the government for redress of grievances, to assemble, and to speak out effectively on issues of public importance would be greatly diminished. Thus, starting in 1958, the Supreme Court recognized a constitutional right of association, finding it rooted in the First and Fourteenth Amendments. Over the subsequent half-century, the Court has fleshed out that right, and applied it in many contexts far distant from the original cases involving Jim Crow state governments attempting to suppress the NAACP.

Supreme Court Decisions

In a series of cases in the late nineteenth and early twentieth centuries, the Supreme Court strongly defended the right of self-defense—holding, for example, that carrying a gun for lawful protection was not evidence of murderous intent, and that a crime victim was not required to retreat or to avoid any place where he had a right to be before he could exercise his right to use deadly force in self-defense. Likewise, the defensive actions of crime victims should not be subjected to judicial second-guessing; as Justice [Oliver W.] Holmes memorably put it: "Detached reflection cannot be demanded in the presence of an uplifted knife."

These cases were decided as matters of federal common law, most of them arising out of death sentences improperly imposed on people in the Indian Territory of Oklahoma for use of a gun in self-defense. Now that *Heller* has made it clear that self-defense is part of the Constitution, and not just part of federal common law, there may be plausible arguments that the rules of the Self-Defense Cases are likewise required as a matter of constitutional law.

Should the Second Amendment be incorporated against the states, a few jurisdictions might have to change hostile procedural rules against self-defense. For example, until recently, Arizona required that a defendant asserting self-defense must carry the burden of proof. The few states which require retreat by a crime victim in her own home might lose constitutional challenges to those laws. If a judge prohibited a criminal defense lawyer during voir dire [jury questioning] from asking potential jurors about whether they had moral objections to self-defense, a criminal conviction from such a jury might be invalid.

Implications for Foreign Law

Heller only applies as binding law within the jurisdiction of the United States. However, American constitutional law has a long record of infiltrating into other civilized nations. American protection for freedom of speech and freedom of the press, as well as American anti-discrimination laws, have had significant influence in our fellow democracies. Sometimes that influence is direct, with foreign courts citing American precedents. But more important, in the long run, is the effect that the American example has on the rights-consciousness of the public in those nations.

Three nations besides the United States have a constitutional right to arms, and twenty nations have a formal constitutional recognition of self-defense.

The right to arms has already shown that it travels. In 2006, the people of Brazil overwhelmingly rejected a referendum to ban gun ownership, and proponents of the referendum noted with dismay the success of anti-referendum advertising which urged Brazilians not to surrender their rights.

For the last decade, the United Nations has led a concerted global campaign against citizen gun ownership. The global prohibitionists have, to the extent they have acknowledged any American interest in protecting American laws, claimed that the Second Amendment protects no individual right of gun ownership, but is only a "collective" right which no individual has a right to exercise. All nine Justices in *Heller* rejected that claim, and affirmed that the Second Amendment guarantees an individual right. As a fallback position, some advocates have stated that the American Second Amendment is unique, and that its very absence shows the permissibility of gun prohibition in other nations.

The latter argument was never really correct as a matter of constitutional law. Three nations besides the United States have a constitutional right to arms, and twenty nations have a formal constitutional recognition of self-defense.

Natural Rights Do Not Depend on Culture

Heller's natural law explication of the inherent right of armed self-defense teaches another very relevant lesson. The right of self-defense is *not* culturally contingent, and it does not depend on national law. The right of self-defense is a universal, fundamental, natural and inherent human right.

Of course there will be many governments which have ignored that right, and will continue to do so. For example, in the United Kingdom and the Netherlands, the principle that there is a right even of *unarmed* self-defense has been in grave danger—at least among the judiciary and the rest of the governing elites.

Yet because *Heller* was not written solely in terms of positive American law, but rather with explicit recognition of preexisting natural rights, the case may play a role in reminding the people of the world that they, too, have "the natural right of resistance and self-preservation," a right which is necessarily effectuated by "the right of having and using arms for self-preservation and defence."

On one side of the debate are the Kenyans who say that the central government, which is manifestly unable and unwilling to protect the tribespeople, should rescind its prohibition on their possession of arms. On the other side is the United Nations, which claims that self-defense is not a right, but is a violation of the right of the criminal attacker, which seeks to outlaw all defensive ownership of firearms, and which has declared that laws in the United States and other nations which allow use of deadly force against rapists and other violent predators are a human rights violation.

Heller points to a resolution of the conflict. Long before there was a United Nations, or a United States of America, there were inherent natural rights. The recognition of those rights is as old as civilization itself. Perhaps one of the greatest influences of *Heller* (and, I hope, its progeny) will be in other nations, where the explicit affirmation of the natural right of self-defense by the most influential court in the world will bolster our global brothers and sisters in their efforts to preserve and strengthen their own natural right of resistance and self-preservation.

3

The National Rifle Association Helped Expand Self-Defense Laws

Erica Goode

Erica Goode is a reporter for the New York Times. *Previously she was assistant managing editor at* U.S. News & World Report.

The National Rifle Association (NRA), a membership organization that promotes the right of American citizens to bear arms, has become very influential in shaping America's self-defense and gun laws. The NRA has successfully pushed for the expansion of self-defense laws and laws that legalize the carry of concealed firearms in states nationwide. The NRA has been instrumental in the spread of Stand Your Ground laws, which remove the duty to retreat when someone is confronted by a threat. The NRA has also fought for the expansion of so-called Castle laws to allow homeowners to shoot or otherwise physically confront intruders not just in their homes but in their yards or vehicles as well. Many politicians are reluctant to oppose the NRA because it is so powerful, and some say that the NRA political agenda— and not citizen need or desire—is driving the expansion of self-defense laws.

No one had yet heard of a Florida teenager named Trayvon Martin when a group of Wisconsin Republicans got together last year (2011) to discuss expanding a self-defense bill before the State Legislature.

The bill, known as the Castle Doctrine, made it harder to prosecute or sue people who used deadly force against intruders inside their houses. But the Wisconsin legislators, urged on by the National Rifle Association [NRA] in a series of meetings, wanted it to go further. They shaped an amendment that extended the bill's protections to include lawns, sidewalks and swimming pools outside the residences, as well as vehicles and places of business.

That expanded bill, passed with little debate by the Legislature and signed in December [2011] by Gov. Scott Walker, a Republican, is the newest of more than two dozen so-called Stand Your Ground statutes that have been enacted around the country in recent years. Those laws are now coming under increased scrutiny after Mr. Martin was shot to death by George Zimmerman, a neighborhood watch coordinator, in late February [2012]. Similar legislation is pending in several other states, including Alaska, Massachusetts and New York.

Laws Vary State to State

Though the laws vary in their specifics and scope, they expand beyond the home the places where a person does not have a duty to retreat when threatened, and they increase protection from criminal prosecution and civil liability. All contain elements of the 2005 Florida statute that made it difficult to immediately arrest Mr. Zimmerman, who has said he shot Mr. Martin, who was unarmed, in self-defense.

Critics see the laws as part of a national campaign by the National Rifle Association, which began gathering on Thursday [April 2012] in St. Louis for its annual meeting, to push back against limits on gun ownership and use. That effort, they say, has been assisted by conservative legislators in states like Wisconsin, and by the American Legislative Exchange Council, which has promoted model legislation based on Florida's law; the council, known as ALEC, is a conservative networking organization made up of legislators, corporations like Walmart, a large retailer of long guns, and interest groups like the rifle association.

In Wisconsin, as in other states, the passage of an expanded self-defense law was helped by the 2010 elections, which vaulted conservative Republicans into office.

The success of the campaign is reflected in the rapid spread of expanded self-defense laws as well as laws that legalize the carrying of concealed weapons. Only one state, Illinois, and the District of Columbia now ban that practice, compared with 19 states in 1981. Bills pending in several states that would allow concealed weapons to be carried on college campuses, in churches, in bars or at other sites would further weaken restrictions, as would either of two federal bills, now in the Senate, that would require that a permit for carrying a concealed weapon that was granted by any state be honored in all other states.

"Both directly and with cutouts like ALEC, the N.R.A. is slowly and surely and methodically working at the state level to expand the number and kind and category of places where people can carry concealed, loaded weapons and use them with deadly force," said Mark Glaze, director of Mayors Against Illegal Guns, a bipartisan coalition of more than 650 mayors that has not taken a position on the Stand Your Ground laws.

NRA Declines Comment

Repeated requests to speak with N.R.A. officials about Wisconsin's law or Stand Your Ground laws more generally met with no response.

In Wisconsin, as in other states, the passage of an expanded self-defense law was helped by the 2010 elections, which vaulted conservative Republicans into office. In Pennsylvania, for example, a Stand Your Ground law passed the Legislature in 2010 but was vetoed by Gov. Ed Rendell, a Democrat. Introduced again last year, the bill was signed by his Republican successor, Tom Corbett.

In Wisconsin, a narrower version of the legislation had languished and died in previous sessions. But with a Republican governor and Republicans dominating both houses of the Legislature, several state lawmakers said that the success of the bill and the expansion amendment promoted by the N.R.A. seemed assured.

"I think it's only normal they assumed this could be their year," said Representative Dean Kaufert, a Republican who introduced the legislation, speaking of the rifle association.

Darren LaSorte, a lobbyist for the rifle association, wanted the legislation, like Florida's law, to extend protection to any place where a person had a legal right to be, said several Republican lawmakers who met with Mr. LaSorte. But having been successful in getting an earlier bill passed to allow the carrying of concealed weapons, Mr. LaSorte accepted a compromise.

"It was almost a 'we'll take what we can get' kind of mode," Mr. Kaufert said. In its final form, the law contained language that closely tracked some parts of the Florida bill.

NRA Urges Citizen Action

In a legislative alert on its Web site, the N.R.A. asked members to "please express your support for this critically important self-defense legislation" and for "N.R.A.-recommended amendments to these bills in order to make the final product a stronger law." The bill, the association said in the alert, "ensures that you don't have to second-guess yourself when defending your home from intruders."

Further, it said, "It also provides civil immunity for good citizens who are acting defensively against violence."

Last year [2011], the N.R.A. spent $97,701 and 627 hours lobbying or engaging in other activities in Wisconsin on behalf of the self-defense law and the concealed carry law, according to the State Legislature Web site.

A lot of politicians are apprehensive to go against the initiatives of the National Rifle Association.

But as in other states, the most powerful weapon the rifle association wielded in Wisconsin was political, not financial. In a state with more than 620,000 registered hunters, the ratings the association gives to legislators could have significant impact on their political fortunes, particularly in the northern part of the state.

"A lot of politicians are apprehensive to go against the initiatives of the National Rifle Association," said Representative Nick Milroy, a Democrat from northern Wisconsin who voted for the concealed carry bill but against the Castle Doctrine. "For a lot of people who are very particular about their gun rights, anything less than an 'A' rating is an antigun stance."

Expansion Amendment Draws Little Opposition

Senator Jon Erpenbach, a Democrat, called the bill a substantial victory for the N.R.A. in the Midwest, where guns have a less central place, say, than Texas. "The N.R.A. did very well for themselves in Wisconsin," he said.

Mr. Erpenbach said he would have voted for the original self-defense bill, which placed a heavier burden on prosecutors in self-defense cases but limited the protection to inside a residence. But he drew the line at the amendment expanding the legislation, he said.

"Who in their right mind could be asking for something like this?" he said he remembers thinking when the measure hit the Senate floor, amendment attached. "If someone takes a late-night dip in your swimming pool, does that mean you should shoot them?"

The fact that the amendment was added by the Assembly Committee on Judiciary and Ethics after the public hearing on the bill, he and others said, prevented it from getting much public attention. And with challenges to collective bargaining, requirements for voter identification and other controversial proposals before them, legislators had a lot on their minds.

"There wasn't a tremendous amount of debate," Mr. Erpenbach said.

The Castle Doctrine legislation . . . was one of a series of bills that seemed to appear out of nowhere as part of some national agenda, rather than arising from concerns of Wisconsin residents.

In fact, at the public hearing, some groups expressed strong opposition even to the far more restricted language of the original legislation. Gregory O'Meara, speaking for the Wisconsin Bar Association's criminal division, said that the division's judges, prosecutors and defense lawyers unanimously opposed the bill as unnecessary and potentially problematic. Wisconsin's existing law, he said, was already stronger than most states, placing the burden of proof on the prosecution to show that a person was not acting in self-defense.

Jeff Nass, president of WI-Force, a Wisconsin gun rights group that works with the N.R.A., and who carries a Glock 20 semiautomatic handgun at all times—"It's a large pistol, but I'm a large person," he said—testified in favor of the bill.

Prosecutors and law professors, Mr. Nass said in a phone interview, "can sit back and analyze in the safety of their chambers what you did and if you did the right thing, but if I kick down your door in the middle of the night, are you going to be worried about it?"

Part of a National Agenda?

Representative Scott Suder, the Republican majority leader, participated in meetings to shape the amendment and said the bill's expansion was not "driven by any group or organization" but came at the urging of other legislators and their constituents.

"We came up with a compromise that did include your car in addition to your home, and that was a fair compromise," Mr. Suder said. "We didn't go as far as some wanted to."

But some legislators said they wondered who those constituents were, other than the N.R.A. The Castle Doctrine legislation, they said, was one of a series of bills that seemed to appear out of nowhere as part of some national agenda, rather than arising from concerns of Wisconsin residents.

Janet Bewley, a Democrat in northern Wisconsin who voted for the concealed carry bill but against the self-defense law, said, "I never heard anyone in this state crying out, 'We must have the Castle Doctrine.'"

4

Castle Doctrine Laws Increase Homicides

Cheng Cheng and Mark Hoekstra

Cheng Cheng is a PhD student in economics at Texas A&M University. Mark Hoekstra is an associate professor and director of the doctoral program in applied microeconomics/labor economics at Texas A&M.

A recent study used state crime data from the FBI to analyze how Castle Doctrine or Stand Your Ground (SYG) laws, which expand the legal justification for using deadly force in self-defense, have affected the homicide rate in states where such laws are enacted. The findings of the study are quite strong. The data clearly shows that the laws lead to more homicides—an 8 percent increase across the states with such laws, which translates to six hundred additional deaths per year. The study also shows that Castle Doctrine and SYG laws do not discourage crime and are not actually a deterrent to burglary, robbery, or aggravated assault, as many people assume them to be. Moreover, the study offers "compelling evidence" that lowering the threshold for the justified use of force results in more of it, not less.

From 2000 to 2010, more than 20 states passed castle doctrine and stand-your-ground laws. These laws expand the legal justification for the use of lethal force in self-defense,

Cheng Cheng and Mark Hoekstra, "Does Strengthening Self-Defense Law Deter Crime or Escalate Violence? Evidence from Castle Doctrine," *Journal of Human Resources*, 48.3 (Summer 2013): 821–853. Copyright © 2013 by Journal of Human Resources. All rights reserved. Reproduced by permission.

thereby lowering the expected cost of using lethal force and increasing the expected cost of committing violent crime. This paper exploits the within-state variation in self-defense laws to examine their effect on homicides and violent crime. Results indicate the laws do not deter burglary, robbery, or aggravated assault. In contrast, they lead to a statistically significant 8 percent net increase in the number of reported murders and non-negligent manslaughters.

A long-standing principle of English common law, from which most U.S. self-defense law is derived, is that one has a "duty to retreat" before using lethal force against an assailant. The exception to this principle is when one is threatened by an intruder in one's own home, as the home is one's "castle." In 2005, Florida became the first in a recent wave of states to pass laws that explicitly extend castle doctrine to places out-side the home, and to expand self-defense protections in other ways. Since then, more than 20 states have followed in strengthening their self-defense laws by passing versions of "castle doctrine" or "stand-your-ground" laws. These laws eliminate the duty to retreat from a list of specified places, and frequently also remove civil liability for those acting un-der the law and establish a presumption of reasonable fear for the individual claiming self-defense. For ease of exposition, we subsequently refer to these laws as castle doctrine laws.

Castle Doctrine Laws Alter Expectations

These laws alter incentives in important ways. First, the laws reduce the expected cost of using lethal force. They lower the expected legal costs associated with defending oneself against criminal and civil prosecution, as well as the probability that one is ultimately found criminally or civilly liable for the death or injury inflicted. In addition, the laws increase the ex-pected cost of committing violent crime, as victims are more likely to respond by using lethal force. The passage of these laws may also increase the salience of the legal protections in place, which may itself affect the decision of whether to use lethal force or commit violent crime. The purpose of our paper is to examine empirically whether people respond to these changes, and thus whether the laws lead to an increase in homicide, or to deterrence of crime more generally.

In doing so, our paper also informs a vigorous policy debate over these laws. Proponents argue these statutes provide law-abiding citizens with additional necessary protections from civil and criminal liability. They argue that since the decision to use lethal force is a split-second one that is made under significant stress, the threatened individual should be given additional legal leeway. Critics argue that existing self-defense law is sufficient to protect law-abiding citizens, and extending legal protections will unnecessarily escalate violence. These potential consequences have been of particular interest recently following some highly publicized cases. In examining the empirical consequences of these laws, this study informs the debate over their costs and benefits.

Study Methodology

We use state-level crime data from 2000 to 2010 from the FBI Uniform Crime Reports to empirically analyze the effects of castle doctrine laws on two types of outcomes. First, we examine whether these laws deter crimes such as burglary, robbery, and aggravated assault. In doing so, we join a much larger literature on criminal deterrence generally. More specifically, however, we join a smaller literature focused on whether unobserved victim precaution can deter crime. For example, [Ian] Ayres and [Steven] Levitt (1998) examine whether Lo-Jack reduces overall motor vehicle thefts, while others have examined whether laws that make it easier to carry concealed weapons deter crime.

We then examine whether lowering the expected cost of using lethal force results in additional homicides, defined as the sum of murder and non-negligent manslaughter. We also examine the effects of the laws on other outcomes in order to shed light on *why* homicides are affected by the laws.

To distinguish the effect of the laws from confounding factors, we exploit the within-state variation in the adoption of laws to apply a difference-in-differences identification strategy. Intuitively, we compare the within-state *changes* in outcomes of states that adopted laws to the within-state *changes* in non-adopting states over the same time period. Moreover, we primarily identify effects by comparing changes in castle doctrine states to other states in the same region of the country by including region-by-year fixed effects. Thus, the crucial identifying assumption is that in the absence of the castle doctrine laws, adopting states would have experienced changes in crime similar to non-adopting states in the same region of the country.

In short, we find compelling evidence that by lowering the expected costs associated with using lethal force, castle doctrine laws induce more of it.

Testing the Assumptions

Our data allow us to test and relax this assumption in several ways. First, graphical evidence and regression results show that the outcomes of the two groups did not diverge in the years prior to adoption. In addition, we show that our findings are robust to the inclusion of time-varying covariates such as demographics, policing, economic conditions, and public assistance, as well as to the inclusion of contemporaneous crime levels unaffected by castle doctrine laws that proxy for general crime trends. This suggests that other known determinants of crime rates were orthogonal [mutually independent] to the within-state variation in castle doctrine laws. Along similar lines, we offer placebo tests by showing that castle doctrine laws do not affect crimes that ought not be deterred by the laws, such as vehicle theft and larceny. Failing to find effects provides further evidence that general crime trends were similar in adopting and non-adopting states. Finally, we allow for state-specific linear time trends.

Results indicate that the prospect of facing additional self-defense does not deter crime. Specifically, we find no evidence of deterrence effects on burglary, robbery, or aggravated assault. Moreover, our estimates are sufficiently precise as to rule out meaningful deterrence effects.

Strong Results

In contrast, we find significant evidence that the laws lead to more homicides. Estimates indicate that the laws increase homicides by a statistically significant 8 percent, which translates into an additional 600 homicides per year across states that expanded castle doctrine. The magnitude of this finding is similar to that reported in a recent paper by [Chandler] McClellan and [Erdal] Tekin (2012), who examine these laws' effect on firearm-related homicide using death certificate data from Vital Statistics. We further show that this divergence in homicide rates at the time of castle doctrine law enactment is larger than any divergence between the same groups of states at any time in the last 40 years, and that magnitudes of this size arise rarely by chance when randomly assigning placebo laws in similarly-structured data sets covering the years prior to castle doctrine expansion. In short, we find compelling evidence that by lowering the expected costs associated with using lethal force, castle doctrine laws induce more of it.

Finally, we perform several exercises to examine the possibility that the additional reported criminal homicides induced by the laws were in fact legally justified, but were misreported by police to the FBI. We conclude on the basis of these findings that it is unlikely, albeit not impossible, that all of the additional homicides were legally justified but were misreported by police as murder or non-negligent manslaughter.

Collectively, these findings suggest that incentives do matter in one important sense: lowering the threshold for the justified use of lethal force results in more of it. On the other hand, there is also a limit to the power of incentives, as criminals are apparently not deterred when victims are empowered to use lethal force to protect themselves.

Policy Implications

These findings also have significant policy implications. The first is that these laws do not appear to offer any hidden spillover benefits to society at large in the form of deterrence. On the other hand, the primary potential downside of the law is the increased number of homicides. Thus, our view is that any evaluation of these laws ought to weigh the benefits of increased leeway and protections given to victims of actual violent crime against the net increase in loss of life induced by the laws.

5

Expanding Castle Doctrine Laws Is a Mistake

Emily Bazelon

Emily Bazelon is senior editor for the online magazine Slate *and a senior research fellow at Yale Law School.*

Prosecutors dislike laws such as the Castle Doctrine because it makes it hard to prove that a person did not commit violence for reasons of legitimate self-defense. The Castle Doctrine does away with the duty of a homeowner to retreat from a threat, even when they easily can, and it makes it far easier to shoot someone and not face legal consequences for doing so. The National Rifle Association has helped get expanded Castle Doctrine laws enacted in more than twenty states by exploiting the unreasonable fear that American homeowners are routinely prosecuted for defending their homes. In truth, the law has always provided for the right of self-defense, and the additional leeway that the Castle Doctrine gives to shooters is both unnecessary and troubling. Castle Doctrine laws encourage violence rather than peaceful solutions, and expanding their use is a mistake.

One amazing thing about the recent spate of laws that make it easier to shoot people and get away with it is how much prosecutors hate them. "It's an abomination," one Florida prosecutor told the *Sun Sentinel*, referring to the state's "stand your ground" law at the center of the tragic killing of Trayvon Martin. And now we're hearing from Montana's county attorneys, sheriffs, and police chiefs, all of whom oppose the 2009 law that expanded the "castle doctrine" to give homeowners more leeway to kill potential intruders. The law is "a solution that had no problem," the president of the Montana County Attorneys' Association said. And earlier this month, the prosecutor for the town of Kalispell cited the newly strengthened castle doctrine in refusing to indict Brice Harper, a man who shot and killed Dan Fredenberg, the husband of the woman Harper was having an affair with. Harper didn't kill Fredenberg at the end of a violent encounter. He killed an unarmed Fredenberg when he walked into Harper's garage.

The idea that Harper won't be charged is crazy making because he had a clear, safe choice that didn't involve shooting. According to the letter Flathead County attorney Ed Corrigan wrote explaining his decision not to prosecute, Fredenberg suspected that his wife, Heather Fredenberg, was having an affair with Harper. On the day of the shooting, she went to Harper's house with her 18-month-old twins to help him get ready to move out. Her husband called to ask if she was with Harper, and she didn't answer. Then she and Harper went for a drive—she wanted to get his opinion about a noise her car was making—and she saw her husband following behind. Harper got out of the car at his house. Heather Fredenberg told him to go inside and not to answer if her husband came to find him. Instead, Harper went inside, got his pistol from his bedroom, and stood at the door from his laundry room to his garage while Fredenberg approached. Harper told the police, "I told him I had a gun, but he just kept coming at me." He also claims Fredenberg was "charging at him, like he was on a mission." When Fredenberg was a few feet away, Harper shot him three times.

Standing Your Ground, for Good or Bad

Harper told the police he feared for his life at that point. Maybe so. But it's hard to see how he could have reasonably had such a fear when he saw Fredenberg walking up the driveway and had the option of going inside and closing the door. Montana's law, however, gives people in this situation more leeway for a confrontation—this really is about standing your ground, for good reason or for bad. You can use force if you think it's necessary to prevent someone from unlawfully entering a house. You can use force "likely to cause death or serious bodily harm" if you think that's necessary to keep yourself from being assaulted. You don't have to fear that you may be killed or seriously injured. You have no duty to retreat or call the police. And if you have evidence that your use of force was justified, it's the state's burden to prove beyond a reasonable doubt that it wasn't.

The larger problem with these Go-Ahead-and-Shoot laws is the insidious way in which they encourage rather than deter violence.

Call me a wimp who's afraid of guns, but I cannot for the life of me understand why you'd want to move from permitting self-defense to encouraging someone to go inside to get a weapon and then lie in wait on someone else approaching their house. I can see why Harper thought Fredenberg would beat him up. I can't see why he put himself in the position of either getting beaten up or gunning him down. Nor is it hard to find other examples in which "stand your ground" or expanded castle doctrine laws let shooters off the hook when their refusal to walk away is integral to the confrontation. . . . [Legal scholar] Jonathan Turley points out that Montana's law led the police to release a man who shot his co-worker at his workplace, the local Wal-Mart.

The response to this week's *New York Times* story about Fredenberg's death and Corrigan's decision not to prosecute includes the claim, from Jacob Sullum of *Reason*, that Harper's decision to shoot would have been justified "even without the changes that the state legislature made to Montana's self-defense law in 2009." Corrigan said the key for him was that the law used to give people the right to shoot to kill intruders only if they entered in a "violent, riotous, or tumultuous manner," but the new version of the law deleted the "violent, riotous, or tumultuous" part. Sullum argues that Fredenberg was being violent or riotous or tumultuous. I don't see it— belligerent, maybe, but not actually violent.

"Go-Ahead-and-Shoot" Laws

And in any case, it seems to me that the larger problem with these Go-Ahead-and-Shoot laws is the insidious way in which they encourage rather than deter violence. The National Rifle Association [NRA], the lobbying force behind the laws, which have passed in more than 20 states, exploits the understandable fear people have of being attacked at home to the point of countenancing killings that are barely provoked at all. The law has always provided for a right of self-defense. As Turley explains, the new breed of castle doctrine is "based on an urban legend that people are routinely prosecuted for defending their homes from intruders." It's one thing to fend off someone who is trying to kill you. It's another thing entirely to set up the legal framework so that if you say you felt in any way threatened, prosecutors have to prove beyond a reasonable doubt that you were wrong.

At least Fredenberg's death has persuaded the local newspaper to call for rethinking Montana's castle law. Now let's see if the legislature is brave enough for a confrontation worth having—with the NRA.

6

Not a "License to Murder"

National Review Online

The National Review Online is a conservative news source that provides commentary on politics, news, and culture.

Both the Stand Your Ground and Castle Doctrine laws serve to protect citizens who defend themselves. Mayor Bloomberg called these laws a "license to murder," but that is not the truth. In most cases where these laws appear to create injustice, it is really the misinterpretation of the law and the subsequent court ruling that is to blame. Although Stand Your Ground and Castle Doctrine have come under fire since the Trayvon Martin shooting, these laws should stay in place and not be repealed.

Since the Trayvon Martin shooting in Sanford, Fla., made headlines, various commentators have called on states to repeal their "Stand Your Ground" and "Castle Doctrine" laws. New York mayor Michael Bloomberg has called Stand Your Ground a "license to murder." However, these laws are reasonable protections for citizens who defend themselves, and in fact they are unlikely to determine the fate of Martin's shooter, George Zimmerman.

States without these laws typically impose a "duty to retreat." This means that when a person is attacked, he may not fight back unless he is unable to get away safely. A Castle Doctrine law removes this duty on one's own property, and a Stand Your Ground law removes this duty in public places, allowing victims to meet force with force. In Florida, victims may assert immunity from prosecution under Stand Your Ground—but they have to prove to a judge at an evidentiary hearing, by a preponderance of the evidence, that they acted in self-defense.

These laws typically include safeguards to avoid abuse. For example, the Castle Doctrine sometimes does not apply to conflicts between two people who live in the same house. And Florida's Stand Your Ground law justifies lethal force only if a person reasonably fears death or serious injury. It also does not apply if the alleged victim was engaged in illegal activity when the attack happened.

It is unsurprising that Stand Your Ground came under fire; when the police initially refused to arrest George Zimmerman, they claimed that Zimmerman's self-defense claim was too difficult to overcome. But the special prosecutor is pressing second-degree-murder charges against Zimmerman, and it seems unlikely that the lack of a "duty to retreat" will affect the outcome.

To justify his claim of self-defense, Zimmerman says that Martin attacked him without provocation, and then knocked him down and beat him. If this is true, Zimmerman had no ability to retreat—and thus would have had no duty to retreat even under the old law. If something else happened to spark the physical confrontation and Zimmerman was the aggressor, his behavior was likely unlawful—a fact that, again, removes him from the protection of Stand Your Ground. The only effect the law is likely to have is to allow Zimmerman to assert immunity on self-defense grounds in a pre-trial hearing, before his case is heard by a jury.

The Martin case aside, some have noted that many prosecutors dislike Stand Your Ground. But as Reason's Jacob Sullum has pointed out, this is unsurprising: The entire purpose of Stand Your Ground is to make it more difficult for prosecutors to obtain convictions in cases where self-defense may have occurred.

For similar reasons, critics are wrong to assume it's problematic when "justifiable homicide" rulings increase following the enactment of Stand Your Ground—in many of these cases, justice was served. What's more, justifiable-homicide trends are not markedly different in states with and without Stand Your Ground, so it's unclear that the law even has this effect. It's also worth bearing in mind that despite doubling over the course of the previous decade, nationwide justifiable homicides totaled only 326 in 2010. The typical year sees 16,000 total killings.

If Stand Your Ground can be further clarified to prevent abuse, it should be, but any law can lead to injustice if its text is blatantly disregarded.

Other commentators have turned to specific cases as proof that Stand Your Ground is problematic. Some of these cases involve murky situations, and the government simply failed to demonstrate that self-defense did not occur.

There have been cases, however, in which Stand Your Ground has led to questionable rulings. In one recent Florida case, a man chased a thief who'd stolen his car radio for more than a block. When the thief swung a bag of radios at him, the man stabbed the thief to death, returned to his apartment to sleep, and later sold two of the radios and hid the knife. Despite Stand Your Ground's requirement that someone reasonably fear death or great bodily harm before resorting to lethal force, and despite its seeming highly likely that the thief was trying to escape with his plunder rather than maim or kill his victim, a judge granted the stabber immunity.

It was immediately clear that the problem was the ruling, not the law: "How can it be Stand Your Ground?" a homicide investigator who worked on the case asked in bewilderment. "It's on [surveillance] video! You can see him stabbing the victim." If Stand Your Ground can be further clarified to prevent abuse, it should be, but any law can lead to injustice if its text is blatantly disregarded.

Simply put, it is unreasonable to demand that crime victims go out of their way to avoid fighting back. Stand Your Ground and Castle Doctrine laws remove that demand, and the case of Trayvon Martin should not inspire their repeal.

7

Stand Your Ground Laws: Do They Put Teens in Greater Danger?

Patrik Jonsson

Patrik Jonsson is the Atlanta-based correspondent for the Christian Science Monitor *newspaper.*

The proliferation of Castle Doctrine and Stand Your Ground (SYG) laws has changed the landscape for today's American teens. Youths have been shot to death in several recent incidents in which these laws were cited as justification. Experts say that Castle and SYG laws are "going to disproportionately result in more consequences to teenagers that are beyond the scope of what the kids were really doing," such as getting shot as intruders for mischievously taking a dip in someone else's swimming pool or sneaking up to a window to visit a girlfriend. There are no data yet on the impact these laws have on teens, but a recent study shows that the general homicide rate has risen as much as 9 percent in states where such laws are enacted. Teens need to be aware that Castle Doctrine and SYG laws significantly increase the danger of participating in stupid pranks and petty crime.

Recent events are raising questions about whether "stand your ground" and "castle doctrine" laws—which offer legal protection to people who hurt or kill someone in self-defense—could disproportionately harm teenagers.

During the past week, three teenagers in states with such laws were shot to death for doing things that, critics of the laws say, teenagers regularly get caught doing.

In Florida, unarmed 17-year-old Jordan Davis was allegedly shot and killed by 40-something Michael Dunn after an argument about a loud car stereo outside a convenience store.

And in Minnesota, retired State Department employee Byron David Smith allegedly wounded and then killed two teenagers, Haile Kifer and Nicholas Brady, who broke into his house on Thanksgiving, apparently on a hunt for prescription drugs.

Though there are no data on the impact of stand your ground laws on teenagers, a Texas A&M University study this summer found that homicide rates had risen by an average of 7 to 9 percent in states that enacted such laws.

This week also saw three teen boys charged with murder in Alabama after their friend, Summer Moody, was shot in April. When a man caught the four breaking into fishing cottages in the Mobile-Tensaw Delta, he allegedly fired a warning shot that killed Summer in what a district attorney called a "tragic accident." On Wednesday, grand jury indicted the three boys, not the man who shot Summer.

"Alabama's law is not quite like Florida's stand your ground law, but it is close," Tommy Chapman, a local district attorney, told *The Mobile Press-Register.*

Especially in the wake of the Trayvon Martin shooting in February, castle doctrine and stand your ground laws are under growing scrutiny. Though they vary by state, the laws are founded on the idea that lawful citizens have no "duty to retreat" from danger in and around their dwelling or even in public. Dozens of states have passed such laws in the past 10 years.

But critics say the laws could significantly raise the stakes for teenagers engaging in stupid pranks and petty crime.

These new laws "are going to disproportionately result in more consequences to teenagers that are beyond the scope of what the kids were really doing," says Kathleen Stilling, a former Wisconsin circuit judge and currently a lawyer in Brookfield, Wis. The worry, she adds, is that teenagers doing things "that are not capital offenses end up facing deadly consequences."

Those dynamics were highlighted by the first test of Wisconsin's castle doctrine law in April, when a teenager fleeing a party busted by police in Slinger, Wis., hid on an enclosed back porch. The startled homeowner shot the "intruder." Prosecutors decided not to press charges against the homeowner.

Though there are no data on the impact of stand your ground laws on teenagers, a Texas A&M University study this summer found that homicide rates had risen by an average of 7 to 9 percent in states that enacted such laws. The causes were not clear, but the authors of the study suggested that "perhaps the most obvious form of escalation—and one most commonly cited by critics of castle doctrine law—is that conflicts or crimes that might not have otherwise turned deadly may now do so."

In Florida, at least, support for stand your ground remains strong. A Quinnipiac poll found that 56 percent of respondents in the state said the law makes society safer. Moreover, a Florida task force convened to look at the law in the wake of the Trayvon Martin shooting said last week that the law may need minor tweaks but is, on the whole, sound.

Trayvon, an unarmed black teen, was shot to death by a community watch volunteer, igniting nationwide protests. His parents are calling for stand your ground laws to be repealed or changed to better protect teenagers.

For Ms. Stilling, the main problem is expanding the scope of the these laws beyond the home.

"When you're talking about the sidewalk immediately outside your house, it seems to me that's going to be an area where there's a higher potential for kids, perhaps naughty but innocent of any destructive intent, could end up," she says. Just talking to teenagers reveals stories "about underage drinking parties, or 'Risky Business' parties, and how everybody ran from the cops and scattered into surrounding yards, where they could end up in a position to frighten someone."

In an opinion article for the *Milwaukee Journal-Sentinel*, she wrote: "I do think that someone needs to tell the kids that the rules have changed."

Pushing the Law Too Far

If the recent incidents raise concerns about an increased danger to teens, however, they also show that prosecutors retain power to take action against those who, they say, misapply the law.

In Florida, Mr. Dunn has been charged with murder and attempted murder. His lawyer says he will invoke stand your ground in defense. Dunn claims he saw a shotgun being raised in the back seat of the car. Neither witnesses nor police report seeing or finding a gun.

In Minnesota, Mr. Smith has been charged with two counts of second-degree murder. While the initial shootings may have been defensible under Minnesota's new castle law, prosecutors said, Smith's decision to shoot the injured teenagers again is likely not covered under the law, since any bodily threat to him had been effectively neutralized.

There Is No Need to Change Stand Your Ground Laws

Dara Kam

Dara Kam is a reporter for the Palm Beach Post *newspaper in Palm Beach, Florida.*

A task force appointed by Florida's governor to assess the state's controversial Stand Your Ground law following the shooting death of Trayvon Martin by neighborhood watch volunteer George Zimmerman in February 2012 has determined that the law is fine as it is and should remain essentially unchanged. Task force members said the law protects honest citizens and that they were confident they made the right assessment in recommending no fundamental changes to the statute. The panel did express concern, however, that those involved in such shootings are currently not allowed to be arrested or detained until an investigation is complete, which can take weeks. The task force will recommend to the state legislature that the arrest immunity issue be addressed, that permissible neighborhood watch actions be clearly defined, that legal training be increased, and other minor clarifications of the Stand Your Ground law.

A panel tasked with looking into the state's "Stand Your Ground" law finalized its recommendations on Tuesday [November 13, 2012] essentially affirming the law and saying that citizens have a right to defend themselves with deadly force without the duty to retreat when they feel threatened.

Gov. Rick Scott appointed the task force in the aftermath of the killing of 17-year-old Trayvon Martin, shot by neighborhood watch volunteer George Zimmerman. Zimmerman said he shot the unarmed black teen in self-defense.

"Clearly, the law is too vague on its face, because you have every Tom, Dick and Harry who shoots anybody now, for any reason, claiming the Stand Your Ground law as their defense," said Benjamin Crump, a Tallahassee attorney representing Martin's parents Sybrina Fulford and Tracy Martin.

Scott appointed the task force, comprised of prosecutors, criminal defense attorneys, law enforcement officials and Palm Beach County Circuit Judge Krista Marx, in response to national protests over the Feb. 26, 2012 shooting and the months that elapsed before a special prosecutor charged Zimmerman with second-degree murder. Zimmerman has pleaded not guilty.

The task force asked lawmakers to limit neighborhood watch groups to "observing, watching and reporting" criminal behavior and said their purpose should not be to "pursue, confront or provoke potential suspects."

But the panel did not make the same recommendation regarding individuals who invoke the Stand Your Ground defense.

"In Trayvon Martin's case, we all believe it's asinine that you can pursue someone, that you can be the aggressor and then shoot an unarmed kid and claim you were standing your ground," Crump said. "Until we fix this law, there are going to be a lot of asinine claims of Stand Your Ground when there's another Trayvon Martin."

Recommendations Sent to Governor and Legislature

Lt. Gov. Jennifer Carroll, the "Citizen Safety and Protection Task Force" chairwoman, said she expects to give the recommendations to Scott and lawmakers before legislative committee meetings begin early in December [2012]. "We've done a very good, deliberate job in our charge in this task force," Carroll said.

Marx, the only judge on the panel, introduced a recommendation dealing with the portion of the law that says a person who uses justifiable force as permitted under the statute is immune from "criminal and civil prosecution."

The panel agreed to ask the legislature to examine whether the law should give killers immunity from arrest or detention during an investigation.

The 2005 law, advocated by the National Rifle Association and signed by Gov. Jeb Bush, removed the duty-to-retreat portion of the self-defense law regarding when the use of force is justifiable.

Since then, investigators and even prosecutors appear to be confused about when they can charge someone who uses Stand Your Ground as a defense, the panel discovered during testimony taken around the state over four months.

"All it did was expand the situations where law enforcement has to make the decision of whether there's probable cause to arrest," Marx said. "It used to be, 'Did they have a duty to retreat?' It was a much more limited circumstance where justifiable use of deadly force would come into play. And now the door's been flung wide open to almost any situation where a person will assert that they were in imminent fear of death or great bodily harm."

The panel agreed to ask the legislature to examine whether the law should give killers immunity from arrest or detention during an investigation.

"I think, from a law enforcement perspective the question is, what does 'criminal prosecution' mean? Does it mean that we can or cannot detain someone? I believe that some law enforcement agencies believe that they are hindered in their investigation," task force member Okaloosa County Sheriff Larry Ashley said.

But the panel did not go far enough regarding immunity from criminal prosecution, Senate Democratic Leader Chris Smith said.

The Immunity Issue

Under the law, "criminal prosecution" includes arresting, detaining in custody, and charging or prosecuting the defendant. And although the panel appeared to agree that the language should be removed, their final recommendation stopped short of that.

Smith, who convened his own panel earlier this year, said he intends to file legislation next week to address the issue.

"That's the number one thing. Law enforcement should be able to detain and investigate. And for them not to address that has me concerned. It just makes me question what they were trying to do," said Smith, a Fort Lauderdale lawyer.

But proponents of the law insisted that it not be weakened.

State Rep. Dennis Baxley, an Ocala Republican who sponsored the law, pointed to Zimmerman's arrest as proof that the law is working and that victims should not have to defend themselves in court.

"Every law abiding citizen needs to know they're not going to have to lawyer up and start defending themselves as if they've done something wrong when they've done something right," Baxley said.

More Studies Lie Ahead

Florida's incoming House speaker, Will Weatherford, told Associated Press he is willing to review the recommendations but does not support major changes to the law. "What we won't do is use that tragedy as an excuse to water down people's ability to defend themselves in Florida," he said.

The task force also asked the legislature to fund a study to find out if the law has been applied unfairly.

What this law is designed to do, and what the law has done . . . is it protects honest citizens.

Miami-Dade County State Attorney Katherine Rundle, who was not present Tuesday, submitted a proposal that included doing away with the immunity provisions and requiring defendants to have to defend themselves in court.

Revoking the immunity provision would fix disparities in how the law is used, said David LaBahn, president of the Association of Prosecuting Attorneys. "To me it's greedy that not only do I have this new right to stand my ground, but I don't even have to go to court. And that's why immunity is so key. I make the decision. I do an act. And then I say I'm immune," LaBahn said after the meeting.

Law Protects Honest Citizens

But that proposal would have gutted the law, said criminal defense lawyer Mark Seiden, who serves on the panel.

"What this law is designed to do, and what the law has done . . . is it protects honest citizens. And it's our job as a task force to protect honest citizens and not coddle criminals," he said. "This law should not be changed."

Former state Sen. Dan Gelber, a former federal prosecutor who voted against the proposal in 2005, blasted the proposal. "They really spent a lot of time and energy to ultimately say and do nothing," he said.

The law is currently being used by criminals "to create a defense that they are really not entitled to," Gelber said. "This was a big wet kiss to criminal defense lawyers."

At the end of the meeting, the task force members defended their work.

"It was a very difficult process where many people had already prejudged the outcome," said vice-chairman R.B. Holmes, pastor of Tallahassee's Bethel Missionary Baptist Church. "We're very clear that we did it right."

Task Force Recommendations

- All people, regardless of citizenship status, have a right to feel safe and secure in our state. To that end, all people have a fundamental right to stand their ground and defend themselves from attack with proportionate force in every place they have a lawful right to be and are conducting themselves in a lawful manner.

- The legislature should clearly define "unlawful activity" as used in the part of the law that says defensive deadly force is not justifiable if the person using it is engaged in unlawful activity.

- Law enforcement agencies, prosecutors, defense attorneys and judges should increase training regarding self-defense laws to ensure fair application of the laws.

- The legislature should define the role of neighborhood watch participants to limit them to observing, watching, and reporting potential criminal activity. The task force said the purpose should not be to pursue, confront, or provoke potential suspects. The law currently does not define participants' roles.

- Regarding the part of the law that says a person using justifiable force is "immune from criminal prosecution and civil action," the legislature should examine the definition of "criminal prosecution" to remove any ambiguity for police to complete their investigation. The law now prohibits "arresting, detaining in custody, and charging or prosecuting" someone who uses justifiable force but it also says a police agency can use "standard procedures for investigating the use of force."

- The legislature should consider allowing innocent third-party victims to sue someone who uses justifiable force. The law now prohibits such lawsuits.

- The legislature should fund a study of how the law has been applied, including variables such as race, ethnicity and gender.

9

Martial Artists Face Extra Legal Scrutiny on Self-Defense

Peter B. King

Peter B. King is a practicing attorney and a Nidan (2nd degree) Black Belt in karate.

Individuals who train in the martial arts must be especially aware of the laws of self-defense and of the potential of their abilities to inflict physical injury. Martial artists are trained in techniques that can cause great bodily harm or death, and using these skills when a lesser amount of force would suffice can bring serious legal consequences. The better trained a martial artist is, the more legally accountable he or she becomes to know the effect of particular strikes and to control the intent with which they are delivered. There are several levels of possible martial response—psychological deterrents without physical contact; pain pacification such as joint locks; counters intended to cause injury and disability, such as blows to the limbs; and counters with significant risk of causing death, such as blows to the head, neck and body—and martial artists face unique legal scrutiny about the appropriateness of their choices when using their skills for self-defense in the public sphere.

When a martial artist reaches the black belt level, he or she should have developed an understanding of the different results to be expected from the use of various techniques. This understanding is needed for the martial artist to

Peter B. King, "Self Defense Responsibilities of Martial Artists," Childerolandsblog, 2009. Childerolands.blogspot.com/2009/08/self-defense-responsibilities-of-marial.html. Copyright © 2009 by Peter B. King. All rights reserved. Reproduced by permission.

comply with the legal and ethical requirement that the use of force in self-defense or defense of others must be limited to that which is reasonably necessary. The use of *excessive* force causing disability or death to the attacker cannot be justified, even when the attacker was in the wrong, and may result in legal consequences to the martial artist. In other words, the degree of response must be proportional to the degree of attack. Instructors of the martial arts have a legal and ethical responsibility to give their students the knowledge needed to form this understanding.

By injuring another with the use of force, one faces both the possibility of being charged with the crime of assault and also being held monetarily liable for the injured person's medical expenses, pain, disfigurement, loss of income, loss of ability to gain income and similar "damages." For significant injuries, these monetary damages could be catastrophic. As these injuries would be deemed "intentionally inflicted" liability would almost certainly not be covered by an insurance policy.

Martial artists are trained to use techniques that may be "likely to cause death" or "great bodily harm," but do they understand that those are the effects of those techniques or the legal ramifications of their use?

The Reasonable Force Doctrine

As the writer is in Wisconsin, references will be made to the legal standards of that state. Similar standards may apply in other states, but laws and the wording of legal standards among states do vary somewhat. The legal standard for use of force in self-defense in Wisconsin is that a person has a right to use the force "reasonably necessary under the circumstances" to defend his person when he reasonably believes that his life is in danger or that he is likely to suffer bodily harm. It is important to understand that the defender (i.e., the martial artist) would have the burden of proving that he acted in self-defense, that the use of some force was necessary and that the amount of force used was reasonable under the circumstances.

Case law holds that oral abuse alone is not sufficient to justify the use of force, however the defender's knowledge of previous threats made by the attacker and any dangerous propensities exhibited by the attacker may, in some cases, justify initiating the use of force to prevent an attack.

The law is not as clear in answering the question of what force a martial artist may use to defend others from physical abuse. The answer to this question would probably depend on a number of factors, such as the ability of the intended victim to defend himself, the relationship of the martial artist to the intended victim, the nature of the perceived threat and the degree of force used to counter it.

Defending Property

The standard for using force to defend one's property, as opposed to one's person, is somewhat different. Wisconsin law categorically states that "it is not reasonable to use force *likely to cause death or great bodily harm* in defending one's property." The term "great bodily harm" is defined as bodily injury that creates a substantial risk of death or which causes serious permanent disfigurement, or which causes a permanent or protracted loss or impairment of the function of any bodily member or organ or other serious bodily injury. The use of "some force" would be allowed if it were reasonable to believe that such force was necessary under the circumstances.

Clearly, martial artists are trained to use techniques that may be "likely to cause death" or "great bodily harm," but do they understand that those are the effects of those techniques or the legal ramifications of their use? Do they receive that knowledge in their training?

What Is "Reasonable" Action?

The word "reasonable" has been used repeatedly in defining the degree of force allowed for self-defense. What is a "reasonable" amount of force to be used in self-defense will vary widely depending upon the particular facts and circumstances of each case. A person who seeks to prove his actions were reasonable will have those actions judged against the standard of what a "reasonable person" of similar abilities, training, knowledge and experience would have been expected to do if faced with the same threatening circumstances. Therefore, a person with martial arts training would be judged against the standard of a reasonable martial artist with approximately the same level of training and skill. A black belt would be expected to have a greater ability to select the specific techniques and the degree of power appropriate to the situation requiring self-defense than would a lower rank martial artist or a person with no martial arts training.

Wisconsin law also holds that the aggressor in a fight is not entitled to fight in self-defense against the person he provoked apart from two situations. First, the aggressor may defend himself if he believes that he is in imminent danger of serious injury or death. Second, the aggressor may re-establish his right to use force in self-defense if he has clearly communicated to the other person that he does not intend to continue the fight but the other persists in fighting.

Degrees of Force

The degrees of force used in self-defense may be analyzed by comparing several levels of threats and counters. . . .

Level 1: Psychological deterrent

An attack may be deterred in some situations without the use of physical force. The appearance of martial bearing, a grimace and even the martial yell (kiai) may be effective in deterring some attacks where the attacker is rational and not deeply committed to the use of violence. A seemingly opposite bearing may also be effective. The martial artist may present an aspect of supreme self confidence and inner calmness (shibumi) that may be very discouraging to an attacker whose goal is primarily to bully and control others. It must be recognized, however, that the use of such deterrents may, in some cases, incite and inflame the irrational or committed attacker to greater use of violence.

Level 2: Pain pacification

In countering an attack, a martial artist may inflict pain upon the attacker and thereby cause him to desist. Typically, the attacker deterred by pain would be one who is attacking impulsively out of sudden anger. It may not be effective on an attacker who is acting out of premeditated malice or with the intent of committing a crime. At this level, the pain would be inflicted by use of techniques that do not fracture bones or otherwise cause permanent injury and disability and that carry a low risk of causing death. The use of throws and joint locks are examples. Kicks and strikes to non-vital areas of the attacker's body may also be effective. Such areas would include the thighs and abdominal region below the rib cage.

Level 3: Counters intended to cause injury and disability

The martial artist may find it necessary to inflict injury and cause disability upon an attacker who cannot be deterred by one of the lower levels. Generally, this attacker would be one who is acting out of pre-meditated, criminal intent or who is acting irrationally under the influence of drugs or alcohol but without the use of weapons or otherwise displaying deadly intent. The degree of injury and disability caused by the defensive counter may be temporary or permanent. The martial artist must appreciate both his own ability to use a technique effectively and the potential for injury at the targeted part of the opponent's body. Areas of the body that may be targeted for injury and disability without significant risk of death would be the insteps, hands, knees, legs and the arms. Strikes to the groin and rib cage may be in this category if done with some moderation.

Level 4: Counters with significant risk of causing death

Legally and ethically, countering with techniques carrying a significant risk of causing the death of the attacker must be confined to situations where it is necessary to deter the potential loss of a victim's life. A prime example would be where the attacker is using a weapon such as a firearm or knife. The use of deadly force to defend one's home against an unarmed intruder is problematical. It may be allowed under the laws of some states, but is not allowed in all. Strikes to the head, face and neck must be seen as always carrying a risk of death. While death will not result in all cases where such strikes are employed, the martial artist must understand that targeting of any vital area of the opponent's body always carries that risk. Blows to the rib cage, in addition to fracturing ribs, may cause injury to internal organs such as the lungs, heart, spleen, liver and kidneys. Injury to any of these organs may result in death. Fracture of the pelvis may easily result in enough internal bleeding to cause death. An added problem in causing injury to internal organs is that there is no effective pre-hospital emergency care for such injuries. External bleeding may be controlled by direct pressure and bandaging; the control of internal bleeding usually requires surgery.

Risks and Responsibilities

A lesson that is taught in most martial arts styles is that any part of the human body may be a target for a blow. (Similarly, it is taught that almost any part of the body may be used as a weapon.) Whether a martial artist learns to use techniques that focus on specific areas of the body as targets, or whether he learns to flail indiscriminately against the opponent's body, he has a deep responsibility to understand the risks involved and the potential for causing serious or deadly harm. . . .

The moral and ethical responsibilities of a martial artist do not end with having successfully stopped an attack with the use of counter force. If the assailant has been injured and further attack is not expected, the martial artist has a further ethical and even legal responsibility to seek emergency medical assistance while rendering reasonable aid to the injured assailant. Aid that can be given to an injured person by another untrained in emergency care may include efforts to clear the airway, protecting the injured person from unnecessary movement and holding a dressing (improvised is fine) over an active bleeding site.

A martial artist forced to use his training in a real-life situation will, in almost all cases, be required to justify his actions in a legal setting.

Ethical and Legal Obligations to Render Aid

Perhaps the most important responsibility would be to call for emergency medical assistance as soon as it is safe to do so. Medical professionals refer to the Golden Hour following a serious injury in which the chances of recovery depend on getting the injured person to definitive medical care, which may often mean into the surgical suite. During that Golden Hour, the injured person's internal compensatory systems are hard at work attempting to keep vital organs viable, however those systems may begin to fail with the passage of time.

Having caused injury to another, if the martial artist failed or refused to call for emergency response and to render reasonable immediate aid to that person, he could be charged with outrageous abandonment and held financially liable for it in addition to any damages caused by using force above the level of reasonable force.

Samurai Code Gives Way to Legalities

The martial arts were developed in cultures that did not have a sophisticated legal system including a reasonable force doctrine, victim's rights and civil litigation for damages. The ethic of the bushido code [the moral code of the samurai] may have discouraged [samurai] and other martial artists from the indiscriminate use of the deadly techniques they had perfected, but it did not impose the degree of legal oversight facing martial artists of today.

A martial artist forced to use his training in a real-life situation will, in almost all cases, be required to justify his actions in a legal setting. This setting may vary from a simple ordinance charge of disorderly conduct, to a criminal charge of assault and battery or even homicide, to a civil lawsuit seeking damages for intentional infliction of injury.

The Consequences of Choices

Martial artists are trained through many hours of self-defense drills, one (or multiple) step drills, katas and sparring to use a huge collection of techniques: strikes, kicks, blocks, throws and sweeps, designed to make forcible contact with various parts of the opponent's body, to overpower him and defeat him. The choice of technique used in training is governed by: 1) the position of the martial artist's body in relation to the opponent's body (front, side, back), 2) the distance between them, and 3) the technique that would logically follow the prior technique just delivered or the block made of the opponent's attack. In law, however, the "proper" technique is governed by one, utterly different standard: the reasonable force doctrine. The consequences of not choosing the correct technique in law can be catastrophic for the martial artist (and the opponent). Every martial artist's fantasy of finally using his training successfully in a real fight to protect himself or other innocents, should be followed by the very real nightmare of being told in a court of law that the techniques he so successfully used do not meet the reasonable force standard and he will either be punished as a criminal or held liable for the opponent's damages.

To be martial artists in 21st century America, we must face the reality of the standards imposed upon us by our society. We must train with knowledge and understanding of the consequences of our art.

10

The Knife-Rights Movement Pushes for More Legal Protection

Richard Grant

Mother Jones contributor Richard Grant is the author of God's Middle Finger: Into the Lawless Heart of the Sierra Madre *and* Crazy River: Exploration and Folly in East Africa.

The Second Amendment protects the right of citizens to bear arms, but it doesn't specifically say that means firearms. Technically speaking, knives are arms, too, and they can be used for self-defense just as readily as they can be used as tools. That's why a group called Knife Rights is pushing to reform the inconsistent and contradictory laws that regulate knives nationwide. Laws about blade length, opening ability, and carrying requirements vary widely from state to state and even from city to city within a state. Simple one-handed folding knives are often inappropriately categorized as illegal gravity knives or switchblades, and even simple knives available at hardware stores have been unfairly demonized. In advocating the right to carry a knife for self-defense or other lawful purposes, Knife Rights makes an argument that is very similar to that of the National Rifle Association: "Weapons don't kill people—people kill people."

Doug Ritter was carrying two pocketknives and a Leatherman on his belt as he entered a suburban barbecue restaurant near his home in Gilbert, Arizona. "If we were in New

York City right now, I could be arrested and sentenced to a year in prison for carrying these knives," he told me as we stood in line at the counter.

Sitting down to carve into a big platter of pork and brisket, Ritter, the founder and chairman of Knife Rights Inc., laid out his arguments for restoring our right to carry switchblades, double-edged daggers, combat knives, bowie knives, stilettos, and cutlasses on any street in America. "Knives are essential tools used by millions of Americans every day, at work, at home, at play," he said. "And on rare occasions, they're also used as an arm in self-defense, or to defend one's family. When the Second Amendment talks about the right to bear arms, it doesn't specify firearms in particular."

Ritter, a 59-year-old survival equipment expert, has carried a pocketknife since he was seven, and he feels naked without one. "It's part of getting dressed, like pulling on your pants in the morning," he said. He started Knife Rights in late 2006 after reading a *Wall Street Journal* article that portrayed military-style tactical knives as a deadly menace but offered no statistics linking them to any crimes.

His group now has more than 2,200 members. Its legal arm receives most of its funding from the knife industry. Its chief lobbyist sits on the National Rifle Association's board of directors, and its website is strewn with overheated endorsements from the likes of [gun-rights activist and rock musician] Ted Nugent ("God Bless Knife Rights!") and NRA executive vice president Wayne LaPierre.

Knives remain regulated by a complicated, contradictory patchwork of state and local laws.

But it might be a mistake to characterize the organization simply as a side project for gun nuts. Knife Rights' board also includes outdoorsman, knife designer, "kitchen despot," and *Joy of Cooking* heir Ethan Becker. "A significant minority of our members are hikers, backpackers, climbers, kayakers, environmentalists," Ritter said. "It's not a left-right, red-blue issue."

Knife Regulations Vary Widely

Sure enough, in 2009, Congress updated the Federal Switchblade Act of 1958, which had outlawed the importation and interstate trade of spring-loaded "automatic" knives amid a panic about youthful hoodlums based on the fictional violence in *West Side Story* and movies such as *Rebel Without a Cause* and *The Wild One*. The bipartisan amendment, signed by President [Barack] Obama, ensured that knives that can be pushed open with one hand—just like the ones on Ritter's belt and an estimated 80 percent of the nonkitchen knives sold in America—are not classified as switchblades.

Still, knives remain regulated by a complicated, contradictory patchwork of state and local laws. That's how it used to be in Arizona: In Phoenix, you could carry a concealed pocketknife, but not a dagger or bowie knife. In neighboring Tempe, knives were banned only in bars and liquor stores. Down in Tucson, you could carry any kind of knife, openly or concealed, just about anywhere except libraries. After a lobbying campaign led by Knife Rights, the state Legislature overturned all these local restrictions in 2010, and Arizonans are now free to stroll down the sidewalk with anything from keychain pocketknives to samurai swords. The same year, the New Hampshire Legislature overturned the state's ban on switchblades, stilettos, dirks, and daggers. In 2011, it voided municipal knife restrictions. Utah and Georgia have done the same.

New York Pushes Back

But Knife Rights has run into sharp opposition in New York City. In 2010, Manhattan District Attorney Cyrus Vance Jr. held a press conference showcasing hundreds of "illegal knives" after his undercover investigators had bought dozens at stores like Home Depot and Eastern Mountain Sports. The stores agreed to pay nearly $1.9 million in penalties. An adviser to Mayor Michael Bloomberg praised the DA for removing "a threat that was hiding in plain sight." Knife Rights is suing the city and Vance for allegedly misclassifying ordinary one-handed folding knives as illegal switchblades or gravity knives. (Gravity knives are not opened by a spring or by pushing the blade out, but rather by releasing a latch that lets the blade "drop" out.)

> It's irrational to believe that if you ban certain types of knives, criminals will somehow stop being criminals.

It's hard to determine whether New York–style anti-knife laws actually make the streets safer. According to the FBI, knives were used in 13 percent of homicides in 2010. Jan Billeb, the executive director of the American Knife and Tool Institute ("Imagine Your Life Without a Knife"), claims that the overwhelming majority of knife crimes are committed with kitchen knives.

"Demonization of Knives"

Ritter worries that if "the demonization of knives" continues, we'll end up like Europe, where knives are often strictly regulated. He recalls a trip to England, where folding blades longer than three inches are illegal and you can't carry any knife in public "without good reason." (Self-defense doesn't count.) Ritter was testing life rafts on a sailboat when the ropes got tangled. "The only practical solution was to start cutting some lines loose," he recalled. "The rest of the folks were all connected with marine safety, but I was the only person that had a knife on board. Not even the captain of this boat. When I pulled it out and opened it up, it was like, 'Oh my God, he's got a knife. Look at that thing!' It was a little three-inch folder, just another tool I carry, and truly a critical piece of safety gear on a boat."

Knife Rights' argument echoes a familiar tenet of the gun rights movement: Weapons don't kill people—people kill people. "A screwdriver makes an excellent weapon if you want to use it that way. So does a baseball bat or a claw hammer," Ritter said, finishing his lunch and putting down his fork and knife. "It's irrational to believe that if you ban certain types of knives, criminals will somehow stop being criminals."

Organizations to Contact

The editors have compiled the following list of organizations concerned with the issues debated in this book. The descriptions are derived from materials provided by the organizations. All have publications or information available for interested readers. The list was compiled on the date of publication of the present volume; names, addresses, phone and fax numbers, and e-mail and Internet addresses may change. Be aware that many organizations take several weeks or longer to respond to inquiries, so allow as much time as possible.

American Civil Liberties Union (ACLU)

125 Broad St., 18th Floor, New York, NY   10004
(212) 549-2500
e-mail: info@aclu.org
website: www.aclu.org

Through activism in courts, legislatures, and communities nationwide, the American Civil Liberties Union (ACLU) works to defend and preserve the individual rights and liberties that the Constitution and laws of the United States guarantee everyone. The ACLU website has an extensive collection of reports, briefings, and news updates related to civil rights issues. Content specifically related to self-defense laws includes the article "Justice for Trayvon," the press release "ACLU Reacts to Murder Charge Against George Zimmerman in Trayvon Martin Shooting," and the blog post "Heller Decision and the Second Amendment."

American Civil Rights Union (ACRU)

3213 Duke St., #625, Alexandria, VA   22314
(703) 807-0242
e-mail: info@theacru.org
website: www.theacru.org

The American Civil Rights Union (ACRU) is a nonprofit dedicated to protecting the civil rights of all Americans by publicly advancing a constitutional understanding of our essential rights and freedoms, including the right to self-defense. ACRU monitors and counters organizations that threaten constitutional rights, and it files amicus briefs in critical civil rights cases. Resources available on the ACRU website include its 2013 brief to the US Supreme Court that argues the right to keep firearms for self-defense is not limited to the home.

Brady Campaign to Prevent Gun Violence (BCPGV)

1225 Eye St. NW, Suite 1100, Washington, DC   20005
(202) 289-7319 • fax: (202) 408-1851
website: http://bradycampaign.org

The Brady Campaign to Prevent Gun Violence (BCPGV) is a nonprofit, nonpartisan organization working to make it harder for convicted felons, domestic abusers, the mentally ill, and others who should not have access to weapons to get guns. Through its advocacy campaigns and network of Million Mom March chapters, the organization advocates for sensible gun laws, regulations, and public policies, and it works to educate the public about gun violence. The BCPGV website features numerous factsheets, studies, and reports about gun control regulations and statistics on gun use, accidents, and self-defense. Of particular relevance to self-defense law is the report "Unintended Consequences: What the Supreme Court's Second Amendment Decision in *DC v. Heller* Means for the Future of Gun Laws."

Cato Institute

1000 Massachusetts Ave. NW, Washington, DC   20001-5403
(202) 842-0200 • fax: (202) 842-3490
website: www.cato.org

The Cato Institute is a public policy research foundation dedicated to limiting the role of government, protecting individual liberties, and promoting free markets. The Institute commissions a variety of publications, including books, monographs, briefing papers, and other studies. Among its publications are the quarterly magazine *Regulation*, the bimonthly *Cato Policy*

Report, and the periodic *Cato Journal*. It offers an extensive selection of materials online, including the article "Self-Defense: An Endangered Right."

Coalition to Stop Gun Violence (CSGV)
1424 L St. NW, Suite 2-1, Washington, DC   20005
(202) 408-0061
e-mail: csgv@csgv.org
website: www.csgv.org

The Coalition to Stop Gun Violence (CSGV) is comprised of forty-eight national organizations working to reduce gun violence. CSGV seeks to secure freedom from gun violence through research, strategic engagement, and effective policy advocacy. CSGV publishes many reports related to self-defense and gun violence, including "shoot first laws," an assessment of recent Castle Doctrine and Stand Your Ground laws, and "Supreme Court and the Second Amendment," an analysis of the *DC v. Heller* US Supreme Court decision.

Karate Law
8000 Towers Crescent Dr., Suite 1350, Vienna, VA   22182
(703) 764-9080 • fax: (703) 764-0014
e-mail: info@karatelaw.com
website: www.karatelaw.com

Karate Law, a law firm in Virginia, specializes in representing martial arts schools, instructors, promoters, and athletes in legal matters pertaining to the use of martial arts, including their use for self-defense outside the dojo (the training facility). The firm's website features a wide array of useful information about the legal issues specific to martial artists, including articles about the use of force, liability, fighting, the legal status of martial arts weapons, and other issues. There is also a useful FAQ section, a glossary of martial arts terms, and links to other websites concerned with the topic.

Knife Rights
313 W Temple Court, Gilbert, AZ   85233

(866) 889-6268 • fax: (480) 496-0282
website: www.kniferights.org

Knife Rights is a nonprofit founded in 2006 to fight against the growing trend of regulating knives, their designs, and their features, and restricting their legally permitted possession and use in cities and states nationwide. The organization gives knife and edged-tool owners an effective voice to influence public policy; encourages safe, responsible, and lawful use of knives and edged tools through education and outreach; and defends knife owners' civil rights through litigation. The Knife Rights website features information about the organization, news updates on knife laws and related issues, and opportunities for individuals to become active with the organization.

National Clearinghouse for the Defense of Battered Women

125 South 9th St., Suite 302, Philadelphia, PA   19107
(800) 903-0111
website: www.ncdbw.org

The National Clearinghouse for the Defense of Battered Women, a nonprofit organization founded in 1987, is a resource and advocacy center for battered women charged with crimes related to their battering. Through its work, the organization aims to increase justice for—and prevent further victimization of—arrested, convicted, or incarcerated battered women. The organization's website features position statements and information and resources about domestic abuse and self-defense, including a series of free online webinars.

National Institute of Justice (NIJ)

810 Seventh St. NW, Washington, DC   20531
(202) 307-2942
e-mail: ojp.ocom@usdoj.gov
website: www.nij.gov

The National Institute of Justice (NIJ) is the research, development, and evaluation agency of the US Department of Justice, dedicated to improving knowledge and understanding of crime and justice issues through science. NIJ provides objective and independent knowledge and tools to reduce crime and promote justice, particularly at the state and local levels. The NIJ website features a wide array of data, graphs, and reports about gun violence as well as topics related to self-defense laws. Articles and reports of note available on the website include "Certain Self-Defense Actions Can Decrease Risk," "Department of Defense Nonlethal Weapons and Equipment Review: A Research Guide for Civil Law Enforcement and Corrections," and "Prosecution Strategies in Domestic Violence Felonies: Telling the Story of Domestic Violence."

National Rifle Association (NRA)

11250 Waples Mill Rd., Fairfax, VA 22030
(800) 672-3888
website: www.nra.org

The National Rifle Association (NRA) is America's largest organization of gun owners and a powerful pro-gun rights group. The NRA's Institute for Legislative Action lobbies against restrictive gun control legislation. In addition to factsheets published by its Institute for Legislative Action, the NRA publishes the journals *American Rifleman, American Hunter,* and *America's 1st Freedom.* The NRA website has a searchable video archive that includes material such as congressional testimony about self-defense laws, NRA position statements, and clips about the Barack Obama administration's stance on self-defense and home protection.

Violence Policy Center (VPC)

1730 Rhode Island Ave. NW, Suite 1014
Washington, DC 20036
(202) 822-8200
website: www.vpc.org

The Violence Policy Center (VPC) is a nonprofit organization that works to stop death and injury from firearms. VPC conducts research on gun violence in America and works to develop violence-reduction policies and proposals. VPC publishes studies on a range of gun-violence issues, and reports available on the organization's website include "A Deadly Myth: Women, Handguns, and Self-Defense" and "Pro-Gun Experts Prove Handguns Are Ineffective Self-Defense Tools."

Bibliography

Books

Carl Brown	*The Law and Martial Arts*. Valencia, CA: Black Belt Communications, 1998.
Tom Diaz	*The Last Gun: How Changes in the Gun Industry Are Killing Americans and What It Will Take to Stop It*. New York: The New Press, 2013.
Joshua Dressler	*Understanding Criminal Law*, 6th ed. San Francisco: LexisNexis, 2012.
Charles Patrick Ewing	*Battered Women Who Kill: Psychological Self-Defense as Legal Justification*. Lanham, MD: Lexington Books, 1987.
Cynthia K. Gillespie	*Justifiable Homicide: Battered Women, Self-Defense and the Law*. Columbus: Ohio State University Press, 1990.
Whitley R.P. Kaufman	*Justified Killing: The Paradox of Self-Defense*. Lanham, MD: Rowman and Littlefield, 2009.
John La Tourrette	*The 37 Secrets of How-To-Beat Up the Bad Guy AND Legally Stay Out of Jail!* Seattle: Amazon Digital Services, 2011.
Andrew Napolitano	*It Is Dangerous to Be Right When the Government Is Wrong*. Nashville, TN: Thomas Nelson, 2011.

David Nash   *Understanding the Use of Handguns for Self-Defense.* New York: Looseleaf Law Publications, 2011.

US Concealed   *Concealed Carry Legal Defense: After*
Carry Association   *You Defend Your Life, Be Prepared to Defend Your Freedom.* Jackson, WI: Delta Media, 2012.

Mitch Vilos   *Self-Defense Laws of All 50 States.* Salt Lake City, UT: Guns West, 2010.

John R. Wright   *Legalized Killing: The Darker Side of the Castle Laws.* Charleston, SC: CreateSpace, 2011.

Periodicals and Internet Sources

Emily Bazelon   "'Stand Your Ground' Promotes Violence," *Monterey County Herald*, October 28, 2012.

Jeffrey Bellin   "How 'Duty to Retreat' Became 'Stand Your Ground,'" CNN.com, March 21, 2012. www.cnn.com.

D.L. Chandler   "Black Community Must Protest Stand Your Ground Law to Protect Black Youth," NewsOne.com, December 6, 2012. http://newsone .com.

John Cloud   "The Law Heard Round the World," *Time*, April 9, 2012. www.time.com.

CNN   "Expanded Self-Defense Laws," CNN.com, 2012. www.cnn.com.

Clayton Cramer and David Burnett	"Tough Targets: When Criminals Face Armed Resistance from Citizens," Cato Institute, 2012. www.cato.org.
Cora Currier	"The 24 States That Have Sweeping Self-Defense Laws Just Like Florida's," *ProPublica*, March 22, 2012. www.propublica.org.
Julia Dahl	"Trayvon Martin, One Year Later: Florida Teen's Death Brings Few Changes to Self-Defense Laws," CBS News, February 26, 2013. www .cbsnews.com.
Judith Browne Dianis	"'Stand Your Ground' Should Be Repealed—Jordan Davis' Death Is Proof the Controversial Law Has an Unjust Impact on Black Boys," *The Root*, November 29, 2012. www .theroot.com.
Christina L. England	"The Battered Women's Syndrome: A History and Interpretation of the Law of Self-Defense as It Pertains to Battered Women Who Kill Their Husbands," *Vanderbilt Undergraduate Research Journal*, vol. 3, no. 1, Spring 2007. http://ejournals.library .vanderbilt.edu.
Amanda Gardner	"More Child Gun Injuries in States with Self-Defense Laws," *U.S. News & World Report*, January 31, 2013. http://health.usnews.com.

Lauren Kelley
: "Are Self-Defense Laws 'Whites Only'?," *AlterNet*, May 8, 2012. www.alternet.org.

Patrick Krey
: "Manslaughter?," *New American*, March 4, 2013.

Marc Lacey
: "Pushing a Right to Bear Arms, the Sharp Kind," *New York Times*, December 4, 2010.

Holly Maguigan
: "Battered Women and Self-Defense: Myths and Misconceptions in Current Reform Proposals," *University of Pennsylvania Law Review*, vol. 140, no. 2, 1991.

Michel Martin
: "When Do Self-Defense Laws Apply?," NPR, November 27, 2012. www.npr.org.

Roland Martin and Keith Beauchamp
: "Do Self Defense Laws Discriminate Against Blacks?," BlackAmericaWeb.com, February 12, 2013. http://blackamericaweb.com.

Chandler B. McClellan and Erdal Tekin
: "Stand Your Ground Laws, Homicides, and Injuries," National Bureau of Economic Research, NBER Working Paper No. 18187, June 2012. www.nber.org.

Evan McMorris-Santoro
: "National Republicans Stand Their Ground on Self-Defense," Talking Points Memo, March 23, 2012. http://2012.talkingpointsmemo.com.

National Rifle Association — "Statement from the NRA on Self-Defense Laws," NRA Institute for Legislative Action, May 1, 2012. www.nraila.org.

J.P. Neyland — "A Man's Car Is His Castle: The Expansion of Texas' 'Castle Doctrine' Eliminating the Duty to Retreat in Areas Outside the Home," *Baylor Law Review*, vol. 60, no. 2, May 12, 2008.

V.F. Nourse — "Self-Defense and Subjectivity," *The University of Chicago Law Review*, vol. 68, no. 4, 2001.

Noah Nunberg — "The Martial Artist's Potential Civil and Criminal Liability," L'Abbate, Balkan, Colavita & Contini, LLP, 2008. www.lbcclaw.com.

Deanna Pan — "New Hampshire House Votes to Repeal Stand Your Ground," Mother Jones, March 28, 2013. www.motherjones.com.

Justin Peters — "Stand Your Ground Is a Terrible Law: Why Do Florida Legislators Want to Expand It?," *Slate*, March 1, 2013. www.slate.com.

Liliana Segura — "Justifiable Homicides Are on the Rise: Have Self-Defense Laws Gone Too Far?," *AlterNet*, November 13, 2008. www.alternet.org.

Mallory Simon and Ann O'Neill   "Unstable Ground: The Fine Line Between Self-Defense and Murder," CNN.com, March 20, 2012. www .cnn.com.

Kenneth W. Simons   "Self Defense: Reasonable Beliefs or Reasonable Self-Control?," *New Criminal Law Review*, vol. 11, no. 1, Winter 2008. www.bu.edu.

Julia Prodis Sulek and Josh Richman   "Gun Control: Are We Safer When Good Guys Have Firearms?," *San Jose Mercury News*, April 23, 2013.

Adam Weinstein   "How the NRA and Its Allies Helped Spread a Radical Gun Law Nationwide," Mother Jones, June 7, 2012. www.motherjones.com.

DeWayne Wickham   "'Stand Your Ground' Law Flaws," *USA Today*, December 4, 2012.

Index